MOVEMENT WITH A PURPOSE

Perceptual Motor-Lesson Plans for Young Children

MOVEMENT WITH A PURPOSE
Perceptual Motor-Lesson Plans for Young Children

Madeleine Brehm and Nancy T. Tindell

*Illustrations by David L. Brehm and
Lynne L. Downs*

PARKER PUBLISHING COMPANY, INC.
West Nyack, New York

Seventh Printing.....March 1987

Library of Congress Cataloging in Publication Data

Brehm, Madeleine
  Movement with a purpose.

  Bibliography: p.
  1. Movement education—Study and teaching (Elementary)
2. Perceptual-motor learning. I. Tindell, Nancy T.
II. Title
GV452.B73   1983   372'.216   83-8023
ISBN 0-13-604629-0

About the Authors

Madeleine Brehm and Nancy T. Tindell have a combined experience of more than 20 years in working with young children.

Mrs. Brehm earned her B.A. in physical education at Southwest Texas University (San Marcos) and her M.A. in guidance and counseling from Our Lady of the Lake University (San Antonio). She has taught preschool, elementary and secondary students for over 11 years and has conducted many professional workshops in the San Antonio area.

Mrs. Tindell earned her B.A. in arts and letters from the University of Oregon (Eugene), and completed her teacher certification at Boise State University (Boise, Idaho) and earned her M.Ed. in Early Childhood Education at Wright State University (Dayton, Ohio). She has taught kindergarten and preschool children and has conducted workshops for teachers in both San Antonio and Fairborn, Ohio.

A WORD FROM
THE AUTHORS

What is one thing hard to get away from? Answer: Your body. It's true! Persons with reading problems can hear the news on TV and persons who dislike math can use the calculator to balance the checkbook, but people with poorly developed motor skills have a hard time circumventing the problem! All through our lives we need to move our bodies through space in an efficient, effective manner. The aim of the lessons in *Movement with a Purpose* is to develop purposeful, joyful, and creative movement to prepare children for a lifetime of healthy activity.

A truly complete program of movement is one that sets time aside for structured and sequentially developed activities for children. It is not our intent to take anything away from free play or recess since both are necessary parts of a child's life. However, teachers and parents cannot easily detect poor coordination on a balance beam while a child is running around the playground! Spotting a student's inability to distinguish right from left is easily missed during free play. Often running and skipping are the basic locomotor skills observed on the playground, but *we* want to look further to see if the child can jump, slide, and hop. Can the child hop on the left *and* the right foot? If so, is the hop a smooth and coordinated action? When bouncing a ball, does the child demonstrate proper bouncing methods? Can the child keep his or her eyes on the ball to catch successfully? All these areas of development are addressed by *Movement with a Purpose*.

We want to develop a student who delights in and takes confidence in moving his or her body and a student who is at home in that body (a necessary building block for a healthy self-concept). A high level of self-esteem for your students is one of our priorities! We need to help a child explore his or her body as well as his or her mind. In learning to use the body, however, the mind will also be opened to new ideas. Whereas a great many theories abound concerning the academic attributes of stressing motor skills with young children, we recommend it for a few simple reasons. It is a well-known fact that children learn and remember most when actively and physically involved in a learning situation. What this means is that we often learn best by doing! Many adults have had the experience of being driven to a new location and then have difficulty finding it again on a second trip. If an individual drives (actively performs the movement pattern), he or she experiences, organizes, and memorizes better the sequences necessary to return to the same location at a different date. Doing the driving necessitates motor activity and motor planning. A child functions in much the same way. Gross motor responses reinforce learning as well as develop coordination.

Movement activities also aid in the formation of a child's body image, which may in turn transfer to the ability to structure space. Eye/hand coordination gained through motor skills should have a bearing on the manner in which a child writes (to express all that intellectual potential). Seriation, the ability to recreate movements in a series, has its counterpart in academic tasks such as spelling and reading. Being judged as a success in games witnessed and valued by peers will help any child's self-esteem to grow...and that child with a positive self-concept may try harder in the intellectual arena as well.

Children today need little physical or muscular effort to function. Very few children knead their bread before breakfast or ride a horse two miles to school. What is required is a high degree of technical know-how to live in our world of computers and machines. For this reason, perceptual motor activities should be taught and proper movement patterns committed to memory. Our children need and deserve a chance to develop their bodies while sharpening their perceptual skills and maturing their neurological systems. They need a well-developed body and well-organized perceptual skills as much as children of other eras. It is our job to provide experiences to promote them, especially when these needed motor activities do not normally comprise a large part of a child's daily schedule. The child is truly victorious when his or her body and mind are working at their developmental best. The child's feeling of success affects everyone with whom he or she comes in contact. How wonderful to know that successful movement skills can help a child sharpen his or her skills in many areas besides the playground. We have provided a program that is not only multi-disciplinary but also a lot of fun! Efficient movement does have a purpose.

Madeleine Brehm
Nancy T. Tindell

About This Book

Movement with a Purpose is a set of perceptual motor-lesson plans for children ages 2½ to 6. Our 32 sequential, developmentally designed lessons expose the student to the joyful nature of movement through gross motor activities. We believe that participation in these activities will enable a child to attain higher levels of body control and encourage higher levels of effort in all areas of school curriculum through growth in self-concept.

Weekly lessons are contained in sets of five activities. Each twenty-minute lesson includes a three-minute warm-up for the total group to prepare for skills being introduced that day. Next come instructions for activities to be taught at *three separate rotating stations*. After the three-minute warm-up, the class is divided into three groups, each working for four minutes at one station. When the teacher gives the signal, students move to the next station for skill practice. By rotating through three stations, students spend more time working on the equipment and less time waiting in lines. More individual attention can be focused on students needing extra help. Each lesson ends with all students working together for a final cooperative game or song, lasting about three to five minutes.

Since each child is an individual who learns and performs at different rates of speed, your lesson may last 15 minutes or stretch to 25 minutes. By closely observing your children, you'll soon discover a comfortable time-frame for your own group. Above all, provide enough time for your children to feel successful.

The "Appendix of Games and Other Activities" at the end of the book should be useful to you. You might want to teach a unit on balance beam skills, mat stunts or ladder work, in addition to weekly lessons. By consulting the appendix, you will be able to develop your lesson plans sequentially. It gives you an overview to help you in selecting a few activities for that special day. A motor skills learning center for your room can also be set up by consulting the appendix.

We strongly recommend following the sequential approach. Introduce a specific movement in the warm-up and let the students practice it in free space. Next, take the movement to the mats, challenging the students to perform in a smaller area. Lastly, introduce the movement on the balance beam, stepping stones, etc., where the movement is executed in its polished form. Such a carefully orchestrated approach assures success. Another feature enabling your students to experience successful movement is the bilateral, unilateral, and cross-lateral format. We want students to have a good foundation in bilateral movement consisting of using both sides of the body in unison before concentrating on unilateral movement. Again, a working knowledge of left and right will be necessary to execute the more difficult cross-lateral movements at the end of the program. Starting a young child out on a difficult cross-lateral movement such as the grapevine would be discouraging and disappointing for both teacher and child. Better to start at the beginning and build the child's skills gradually.

Our first twelve lessons develop *bilateral movement* involving both sides of the body working together. The next nine lessons focus on *unilateral movement,* isolating right and left sides of the body. Awareness of right and left is an important concept for students. Final lessons highlight *cross-lateral movement.* These movements are the most difficult and thus placed last after the student has had time to develop sufficient body coordination. Cross-lateral movement is most appropriate for four- and five-year-old students. Younger two- and three-year-olds having difficulty with cross-lateral lessons will profit by a return to the bilateral lessons for additional practice.

Although this program is the result of many years of teaching experience, it should not be the final word in your motor skills program. As each teacher adds his or her own special touch to the presentation of lessons, *Movement with a Purpose* becomes a more valuable tool. Feel free to deviate from or repeat lessons as you see fit. Be creative and allow your students to be creative too. Most importantly, help your students develop joyful, purposeful movement. We wish you happy, motivated, and enthusiastic students!

LEWIS COUNTY HEAD START
P.O. BOX 266 - 206/497-3346
RANDLE, WA 98377

HOW TO SUCCEED IN
MOVEMENT WITH A PURPOSE

The following presents practical information and recommendations for using the perceptual motor-lesson plans in this book. Included are:

- guidelines for teaching the various activities
- brief, illustrated directions for using rotating stations with groups of children
- definitions of the vocabulary associated with movement
- a list of equipment needed together with specifications for its construction
- an informal screening device to help you identify children's specific strengths and weaknesses in motor skills before they begin the program

These should simplify your preparation and teaching tasks and help to ensure the greatest effectiveness of the activities for your students.

Teaching Guidelines

The authors encourage all participants, teachers and parents, to follow these guidelines in order to receive the most benefit from this program of developmental activities. *Please try to:*

1. Guide children through the stations.
2. Become familiar with the instructions before presenting them to the children.

3. Be flexible and change your approach to suit students' ages and experience.

4. Let students be successful. Practice activities many times. Instant success is not guaranteed, but practice makes perfect!

5. Encourage students to create new activities.

6. Allow students extra time if the lesson seems to demand increased concentration.

7. Bypass an activity if it is not working with your particular group. Remember: everybody is different.

8. Add more stations if you are working with a large class.

9. Give plenty of support and praise.

10. HAVE FUN!

Using Rotating Stations

The use of rotating stations is an important asset to this activities program. Each lesson gives children the opportunity to perform three or more different developmental skills, and rotating stations keep them from waiting in lines to perform the skills. The stations also give you the benefit of watching the children perform more often and make it possible for you to provide individual help when needed.

After the initial three- to five-minute warm-up activity in each lesson, give students a quick demonstration of the activities that will be performed at each rotating station. Then divide students into three groups and direct each group to a different station. For example, group 1 might go to the stepping stones station, group 2 to the scooters station, and group 3 to the balance beam station. After four or five minutes, have the students move on to another station to practice a different skill. Remember to place stations in a circular arrangement so children can *watch each other* too!

A typical lesson will take approximately twenty minutes, including a three-minute warm-up, four minutes each at three rotating stations, and five minutes for the closing game.

Three Separate Rotating Stations

Movement Vocabulary

Knowledge of movement vocabulary will help you appreciate more fully the benefits children will receive from the various activities throughout *Movement with a Purpose*.

agility capacity for fast reaction in body movement

auditory acuity responding to an overt stimulus (*example:* listening to a bouncing ball)

balance the ability to make continuous and accurate adjustments of the body with a minimum of support

(a)dynamic balance—balance during locomotion
(b)static balance—balance while stationary

bilateral movement that uses both sides of the body in simultaneous or parallel movement

concept of fixation the eyes' ability to maintain focus upon an object

cooperation working together to reach a goal

cross lateral simultaneous movement of the opposite sides of the body (*example:* right arm and left leg moving or striking together)

directionality the projection of self in space and the understanding of the direction that one needs to take in space to achieve a task

eye/hand coordination ability to use the eyes and hands together to accomplish a purpose

gross motor coordination arises from organization of the large muscle system to achieve purposeful body movement

kinesthetic awareness the awareness of one's body in space, either stationary or in motion

laterality the conscious awareness that the body has two sides—a right and left—and the ability to control the two sides together and separately

motor planning involves perceiving a pattern of movement and organizing body to achieve that movement (a true intellectual challenge)

perceptual motor skills those skills involving the receiving of information through the senses and the ability of students to receive, plan, and react to that information

spatial awareness understanding of where one is in space —how close or how far objects in space are in relationship to one's own body

tactile awareness sense impressions (touching and feeling) received as a result of direct contact with objects

unilateral movement isolating one side of the body

Equipment Needed

The following is a complete list of the equipment required to carry out the various activities in *Movement with a Purpose*, together with the specifications for making your own coordination ladder, stepping stones, jump box and incline board, step launcher, scooter, and balance beam.

1 balance beam
1 jump box with incline board
2 scooter boards
2 step-launchers
1 coordination ladder (approximately 14 inches between rungs)
5 balls (6 to 8 inches in diameter)
5 hoops or bicycle tires
4 traffic cones
stepping stones taped to floor
beanbag for each student
mats or soft surface for safety
rope (lightweight, approximately 6 feet in length)

Specifications

Coordination Ladder

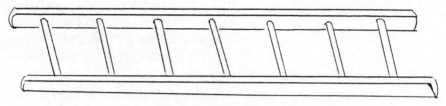

Rails: 2" by 4" by 8'
Rungs: 1-5/16" dowel, 14" apart

Stepping Stones

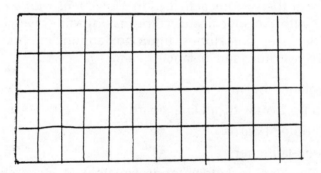

Squares: 14" by 14"

NOTE: *These may be: (1) taped to the floor with masking tape, (2) taped to a large piece of vinyl, or (3) painted permanently on the playground or the gym floor.*

Jump Box and Incline Board

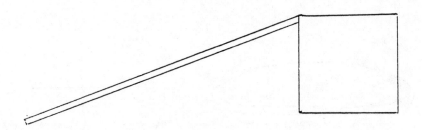

Board attaches securely to box with 2" hooks.
Box is about 20" high and 15" square.
Incline board is plywood the width of box by 48" by 3/4."
Top of box and incline board may be covered with carpet.

Step Launcher

30" long
5"wide
2" by 2" dowel or square placed 10" from end

Scooter

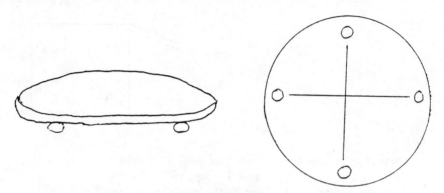

17" in diameter
4 rubber casters good for all surfaces

NOTE: *We use furniture casters, 1-5/8" to 2" in diameter. The board is easy to acquire in the form of an old sink cut out from a counter top. Hardware stores sell them for about $2. There is no need to change the size.*

Balance Beam

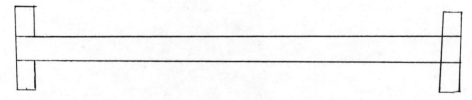

Beam 2" by 4", 6' in length, approximately 3" off ground

Informal Screening of
Perceptual Motor Skills

Before starting a student in motor skills lessons, it is a good idea to have some knowledge of the child's functioning level. For this reason we recommend the *informal* screener on the following page. It will give you a baseline behavior level in different areas so that you will be able to see improvement as the year progresses.

It is important to note that this is an informal screener designed to show strengths and weaknesses, not right or wrong. There is no norm or recommended level a student should reach. This device simply provides awareness of where a child is beginning. If a child exhibits great difficulty, that is an indication that he or she needs more exposure to gross motor activities.

INFORMAL SCREENING OF PERCEPTUAL MOTOR SKILLS

Name: _____   Age: _____

1. Can the student walk a 10-foot line taped to the floor heel-to-toe without stepping off the line? How many steps did the child take before stepping off? (_____steps) ____ **YES** ____ **NO**

2. Can the student walk cross-step along a 10-foot line taped to the floor? (The student will stand with the left foot on the right side of the line and the right foot on the left side of the line and walk forward continually crossing foot over foot.) _____ **YES** _____ **NO**

3. Can the student use both sides of the body to balance? (The student will walk on the line heel-to-toe using the opposite arm and foot, the right foot stepping and the left arm out in front of the body. Please note that this cross-lateral task will naturally be difficult for two- and three-year olds.) ____ **YES** ____ **NO**

4. Can the student use both hands to screw on a large nut and bolt? (This gives a good indication of eye/hand coordination.) Can the student perform this task with eyes closed? ____ **YES** ____ **NO**

5. Can the student identify each body part: eyes, feet, shoulders, wrists, knees, elbows, chest, and back? (Underline missed parts.) ____ **YES** ____ **NO**

6. Can the student duplicate a simple pattern with slow, persistent control? *Examples:*
   (a) clap, slap knees, clap, slap knees
   (b) double jump in stepping stones (p. 35)
   (c) side to side jumping through two sets of stepping stone lanes
   ____ **YES** ____ **NO**

7. Have the child jump forward with both feet together and land without losing balance. (Measure the distance of the jump.)

   Distance of jump:
   _____

8. Have the child jump from a chair or box 15 to 20 inches high.
   Does the child land with both feet together or with one foot landing before the other?

   Both feet? _____
   Which foot landed first?
   Left _____
   Right _____

9. Have the student sit on the floor with hands resting at sides. How *slowly* can the student move his/her hands above the head? (30–45 second timing)

   Time/Seconds:
   _____

10. Can the student stand on one foot for 30 seconds? (Right foot and left foot)

    Time/Seconds:
    Left _____
    Right _____

Contents

CROSS-LATERAL MOVEMENTS: Using both sides of the body in opposition, crossing the midline

BILATERAL MOVEMENTS

Using both sides of the body working together

The first type of movement we will explore is bilateral movement. Bilateral movements involve both sides of the body working simultaneously. The action may be in the hands while clapping, for example, or in the feet while jumping. The whole body becomes involved when we teach jumping jacks. It is a natural movement with which to begin a motor skills program as it comes easily and naturally to most children. Bimanual dexterity (use of both hands) is an important step in achieving sensorimotor control. Indeed, successful use of both sides of the body in gross motor tasks plays a great part in developing the young child's brain.

Bronco (Creative Movement Lesson)

WEEK 1

WARM-UP

Promotes: Body image, laterality.

Activity:

(1) *Finding space:* Students jump forward, backward, right, left, up and down. "Move in your own space and watch out for your neighbor!"

(2) *Body image:* "Do as I do. . . ." Class names body parts as they are touched with *both* hands.

(3) *Arm circles:* Students raise arms out to the side and make large and small circles with both arms, forward and backward, fast and slow. Have them try this with heads tilted back and then tilted forward, chins on chests.

NOTE: *Placing students on carpet squares or in hoops helps students to understand the size and limitations of their own space.*

BALANCE BEAM

Promotes: Balance, directionality, body awareness.

Need: Balance beam.

Activity:

(1) Student walks forward to middle of beam, makes quarter-turn to right or left, rises on toes, lowers, and walks the rest of the beam. Arms are out for balance if necessary.

(*Hint:* For the quarter-turn, suggest the student turn to make feet point to the wall, door, or some such object, rather than asking for a "quarter" turn.)

(2) On beam, student balances on one foot (left and then right).

(3) Student does half- and full-turn on beam.

Activity #3

STUNTS

Promotes: Gross motor coordination, laterality.

Need: Mats desired, but not necessary.

Activity:

(1) *Standing broad jump:* Students jump with both feet forward, sideways, and backward. Stress fluid body motion. Arms can swing.

(2) *Burpee:* Four counts: (a) Place hands on floor; (b) push feet out in "push-up" position; (c) bring feet back to hands on floor; (d) stand up with hands on hips.

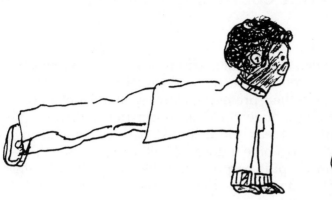

Burpee

STEPPING STONES

Promotes: Body control, balance and motor planning.

Need: Stepping stones.

Activity:

(1) The student jumps from one square to the next with both feet in the same square. Emphasize body control and balance. Slowly and carefully work for feet landing together. You should hear a "thump," rather than a "thump–thump."

(2) Students jump with right foot in right square and left foot in left square.

(3) Students jump with right foot in right square and left foot in left square backwards.

NOTE: *Try using masking tape or bookbinding tape to place stepping stones on floor or carpet. If stepping stones cannot be left on floor, try using a large carpet remnant and taping the stepping stones on the remnant. It can be used and then rolled up and put away.*

CREATIVE COOPERATIVE MOVEMENT

Activity:

Balloon game: Group holds hands in a circle and clusters very close to center. Teacher and students blow and blow and blow until their pretend balloon is all inflated and the children are in a huge circle, arms outstretched. Then the balloon springs a leak and it shrinks back to deflated size. Next, children become individual balloons and the teacher blows them up puff by puff until they are light and airy. Then they POP and deflate to a crumpled heap on the floor. Students love this one!

WEEK 2

Promotes: Body image, spatial awareness.

Activity:

(1) *Finding space:* Students jump forward, backward, right, left and up in their own space.

(2) *Arm circles:* Students raise arms out to the side and make large and small circles, forward and backward, faster and slower.

(3) *Five-count rhythm:* Clap and tap head, clap and tap shoulders, clap and tap stomach, clap and tap knees, clap and tap toes. Touch toes again and reverse. Work up to a rhythm. Teacher recites the words with students: "Clap and tap head. Clap and tap shoulders, etc." Students will not only work up to a rhythm but a new song. Students can add more body parts on their own.

STEPPING STONES

Promotes: Gross locomotor coordination, eye/foot coordination.

Need: Stepping stones.

Activity:

(1) *Double jump:* Student moves from square to square with a double jump in each square. Try jumping with student. If necessary, jump holding student's hand. Say, "Big jump, little jump, big jump, little jump, etc." (*Hint:* Jump to the square with a big jump and then jump in the square with a little jump. It is like jumping rope.)

(2) Student takes double jump backwards and continues to the end of the stones. Be sure that student places both feet down at the *same* time.

(3) Student hops or jumps to land on the taped line on each square all through the stepping stones.

BALANCE BEAM

Promotes: Balance, spatial awareness.

Need: Balance beam, yardstick.

Activity:

(1) *Step-over stick:* Student walks forward to center of beam and steps over yardstick held by friend or teacher about six inches above beam. Student walks to end of beam.

(2) Student walks backward to center of beam and steps over yardstick.

Challenge:

(1) Student walks in a side-stepping motion over the stick.

(2) Student stands by side of beam and jumps over the beam.

Challenge #2

STUNTS

Promotes: Balance, laterality, coordination.

Activity:

(1) *Bunny hop:* Student assumes squat position and puts hands on floor. He or she moves hands forward together and then follows with feet jumping together. Student moves along floor jumping first hands and then feet.

(2) *Chase the rabbit:* Student puts hands on floor, pushes feet alternately out to push-up position and returns them to squat position under the chest. Try having students accomplish sets of five at a time.

Challenge:

(1) Students sit on floor tailor fashion and stand up without using hands.

Bunny Hop

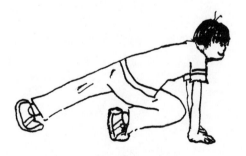

Chase the Rabbit

GAME

Activity:

(1) *Big jump, little jump:* To the tune of "Teddy Bear, Teddy Bear."

"Big jump, little jump, turn around.
Big jump, little jump, touch the ground.
Big jump, little jump, give your legs a slap.
Big jump, little jump, give the ground a clap.
Big jump, little jump, put your hands in your lap."
(Sit down)

(2) *Bunny hop:*

"Bunny bunny, hop hop fast.
Bunny bunny, hop hop slow.
Bunny bunny, reach up high.
Bunny bunny, crouch down low.
Bunny bunny, turn around.
Bunny bunny, sniff the ground.
Bunny bunny, you're the best.
Bunny bunny, give yourself a rest."

(Sit down)

WEEK 3

Promotes: Laterality, gross motor coordination.

Need: Hoops or bicycle tires.

Activity:

(1) Student finds own space in which to work by exploring the space in front, back, to the right and to the left to be sure it is empty. We want students to have a safe, private space in which to work. Young students profit from use of a hoop to define their space until they learn how to self-space properly.

(2) *Jumping jacks:* Isolate movements. First show hand movement, then foot movement, and finally work to combine the two together. Emphasize slow, careful movement. Use the terms "open" and "close" to describe movements of hands and feet.

(3) Students stand on right foot and hop in a circle. Then they stand on left foot and hop in a circle. (Two-year olds may stand on one foot, lift it to knee level and put it down; then lift the other foot to knee level and put it down.)

BALANCE BEAM

Promotes: Laterality, spatial awareness, self-confidence, strong leg muscles.

Need: Balance beam.

Activity:

(1) *Jump on beam:* Student stands on one side of the beam, jumps up on the beam and maintains balance. Student jumps down and repeats activity five times. This is very difficult, but important to show students where in space the beam really is. Some students may step up and jump down. Teacher may stand on opposite side of beam, arms extended, palms up. Student places palms on teacher's palms and jumps. This serves to steady the student and helps his or her confidence.

(2) After fifth jump, student walks backwards off the beam.

(3) *Lame walk:* Student walks with one foot on beam and one foot on floor. This will strengthen legs for jumping and hopping later.

LADDER

Promotes: Problem-solving skills and dynamic balance.

Need: Ladder.

Activity:

(1) Student *jumps* forward *between* rungs of ladder.

(2) Student walks forward balancing on rungs of ladder only, without touching floor.

(3) Student walks backward between rungs ... no peeking!

Challenge:

(1) Student jumps backward between rungs.

(2) Student walks on one rail of ladder.

Challenge #2

STUNTS

Promotes: Laterality, gross motor coordination.

Activity:

(1) *Monkey:* Student squats down with hands on floor. Hands move to the side one jump and feet follow. This animal movement should be executed as two distinct movements.

Monkey

Hint: Colored carpet squares placed in two horizontal lines will help students know where hands and feet should move.

(2) *Bronco:* Student squats down with hands on the floor and kicks feet up high into the air like a bucking bronco. Object is to bring feet down *together* to the floor for a coordinated landing.

Bronco

CREATIVE MOVEMENT LESSON

Activity:

(1) Children achieve self-space in which to work: "On starting signal, move one hand around you to as many places as you can find." Teacher gives signal to start, students move hands and then teacher signals to "Freeze." Be sure to use right and left hand and foot for all activities.

(2) "How many places can you take one foot without having to touch the floor?" Students move feet until signal is given to *freeze*.

(3) "How many places can you take one hand and one foot at the same time without having them touch the floor?" Switch hands and feet and repeat. Try with same hand and foot and then with alternate hands and feet. Teacher may focus on a few interesting poses.

WEEK 4

Promotes: Strong back, shoulder, and abdominal muscles.

Need: Ball.

Activity:

(1) Students determine own working space where they have enough room to stretch out comfortably.

(2) Students close eyes and clap as they hear the sound of the ball being bounced slowly by the teacher. Students turn their backs and repeat activity. This discourages peeking!

(3) Students lie on back. They sit up as they hear the sound of the ball being bounced.

(4) *Airplane:* Students lie on stomach, lift legs off floor, relax. Then students lift arms straight out. Combine both moves at the same time. (*Hint:* Remind students to keep knees straight and heads up. This posture is excellent for back, legs, and abdominal strength.) This airplane ride is lots of fun. Ask where the class wants to go and then "take off" and "land" together. Encourage lots of airplane motor noise!

BALL REACTION

Promotes: Precise body reactions, auditory acuity.

Need: Ball.

Activity:

(1) Teacher or student bounces ball as students, with eyes closed, jump to the sound of the ball. Try one bounce first, then two, three, four.

(2) With eyes closed, students jump to varied heights, interpreting the height of the bounce.

(3) Students sit on the floor and roll ball to each other. They can count how many times it is rolled to them before the station time is up.

BALANCE BEAM

Promotes: Dynamic balance, problem solving.

Need: Balance beam, yardstick, hoops.

Activity:

(1) Student walks forward, hands overhead, while carrying yardstick using an overhand grip with hands placed slightly wider than shoulder distance apart.

(2) Student moves yardstick out in front of chest and repeats action. Stress good posture with head up. Walk slowly.

Challenge:

(1) Place hoops or bike tires on one end of yardstick, while student holds the other end. Walk forward on beam.

NOTE: *Students learn balance by imbalance. This activity will force them to adjust their center of gravity and to become more aware of how to bring their bodies back into balance.*

LADDER

Promotes: Strengthens shoulders, arms and back, tactile awareness.

Need: Ladder.

Activity:

(1) Student crawls forward on hands and knees in spaces between rungs.

(2) At the end of the ladder, student stands and walks backward *on rungs* of ladder. A partner may hold hands for help in balancing.

Challenge:

(1) *Seal walk:* Student places hands on rail or rungs and pulls body along ladder, legs extended behind.

(2) Student walks on rail up and down ladder.

NOTE: *Please explain the parts of the ladder to students. The ladder has two rails and six or seven rungs and spaces between the rungs.*

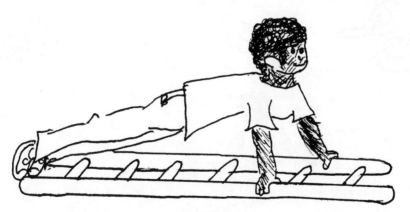

Seal Walk

GAME

Activity:

Jumper Ball: Students sit in two circles of about ten children each. Jumper stands in middle, eyes closed. Roller rolls the ball at jumper's feet and calls "jump" when ball is about to hit jumper's feet. Jumper jumps over the ball and turns to face the person who has caught the ball. Jumpers get three jumps and then the last person holding the ball gets a turn being the jumper.

NOTE: *A lot of trust is needed in this game. Some students have a hard time keeping their eyes closed, although this is necessary for practicing auditory acuity. If the student lacks the skill or the trust, allow the student to keep eyes open until more confidence and skill develop.*

Jumper Ball

WEEK 5

WARM-UP

Promotes: Laterality, gross motor coordination.

Activity:

    (1) *Airplane:* Students lie on stomach and lift legs off floor, then lift arms off floor. Combine both moves.

    (2) *Angels in the snow:* Students lie on back and slide arms along floor from sides to above the head, touch hands and bring back to sides. At the same time, legs slide open and closed. It is similar to a jumping jack. Some areas of the country get no snow so this activity might call for a little teacher alteration. Angels can also be made in the sand at the beach or in the sandbox in the yard.

    (3) *Coffee grinder or pepper mill:* One hand on floor supporting weight. Legs out to side. Walk around the hand on the floor, other hand out for balance if needed.

LADDER

Promotes: Laterality, balance, gross motor coordination.

Need: Ladder.

Activity:

    (1) Student runs between rungs.

    (2) Student walks forward with one foot on each rail, balancing carefully.

Challenge:

(1) Students jump sideways between rungs.

(2) Students jump two times between each rung, sideways (double jump). It helps to count, "one, two" in each space. Students' feet should always be facing the rails of the ladder.

Challenge #2

BALANCE BEAM

Promotes: Spatial awareness, body image, dynamic balance, concept of fixation.

Need: Balance beam, yardstick; triangle, square or zigzag shapes.

Activity:

(1) Student looks at one object at eye level at end of beam while walking on beam (teacher's hand or yardstick is held parallel to floor). To keep their attention at eye level, teacher can hold up one, then four, then two fingers and students call out the number. Or, teacher can hold up color or shape cards and younger students name the colors and shapes as they walk.

(2) Student looks at eye level object at side of beam while walking on beam.

Challenge:

(1) Student walks forward on beam while tracing the outline of a triangle, square, or zigzag pattern with index finger. Shape is held at eye level at end of beam by teacher.

(2) Student walks sideways on beam while tracing the outline of a triangle, square, or zigzag pattern with index finger. Shape is held at eye level at side of beam by teacher. Teacher should watch for eyes fixating on shape and concentration to task.

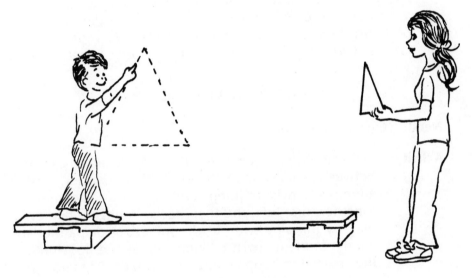

Challenge #2

BEANBAGS

Promotes: Dynamic balance, eye/hand coordination, eye/foot coordination.

Need: Two hoops and four beanbags.

Activity:

(1) Student balances beanbag on head and walks around one hoop.

(2) Student stands in one hoop and teacher or student stands about two feet away, holding second hoop on edge. Student uses underhand toss to throw the bag through the hoop, and student retrieves the bag by walking through the hoop without touching it. Student throws overhand at next turn.

Challenge:

(1) Student places beanbag on foot, shoulder, or knee and throws it into hoop.

NOTE: *Directionality, eye/hand control and spatial awareness are practiced when students have the opportunity to throw at a variety of targets: tall, vertical targets; wide, horizontal targets; and circular targets.*

COOPERATIVE GAME

Need: One beanbag per child and three hoops.

Activity: *Beanbag twist:* Each student holds beanbag tightly between knees, joins hands with a partner, and attempts to twist or jump across the floor. Feet move together, first toes and then heels. Younger children may try jumping without dropping bag or partner's hands. Students twist or jump across the floor until they reach the hoop where they drop the bag into the hoop. As each student succeeds, the teacher congratulates him or her on reaching the goal. These students may now watch and help other students. For example, they can pick up the beanbag if it drops. Teacher can then ask, "How many times were you a good helper?" This is a great activity to do to music with a "bouncy beat."

WEEK 6

Promotes: Body image, gross motor coordination.

Activity:

(1) *Body identification with a partner:* Students find a partner and hold hands. Teacher calls out body parts such as back, arms, legs, hands, head, neck, elbow, etc., and children touch them *on partner.* Older children can close eyes while playing.

(2) *Giggling body identification:* Keeping the same partners, students follow teacher's new directions. "Stand back to back, bottom to bottom, elbow to elbow, knee to knee, nose to nose, etc." This is a great cooperative activity and is a sure-fire giggle-getter.

(3) *Gallop:* Run with one foot leading at all times. Perhaps students can gallop to their first station.

BALANCE BEAM

Promotes: Dynamic balance, gross motor coordination, concept of fixation.

Need: Balance beam with beanbag placed in the middle, yardstick.

Activity:

(1) Student walks to middle of beam, picks up the beanbag and places it on head, shoulder, elbow or back of hand and walks to the end of the beam. Student then replaces the bag for the next participant. (*Hint:* Placing bag on shoulder or back of hand is the easiest.)

51

(2) Student gallops to end of the beam with both hands holding yardstick between legs like a stick horse.

(3) Student stands sideways on beam, bends knees to a squat position, stands straight up, takes two side steps. Student repeats this squat position, stand and step pattern to end of beam.

Activity #3

Challenge:

(1) Student walks on beam with one foot directly in front of the other, heel touching toe. Student or teacher stands at end of beam, holding up index finger moving in rotary (circles) fashion. The student on beam (without moving head) continues to walk while eyes are following index finger. Motion should be made large and slowly.

JUMP BOX

Promotes: Self-confidence, agility.

Need: Jump box, mats, grass or rug on which to land.

Activity:

(1) Student walks up the incline board onto the jump box, takes proper jumping position with knees slightly bent and jumps off with both feet at once to land without falling. Landing on balls of feet is important to avoid shin splints. Landing with flat feet may hurt!

NOTE: *The teacher must stand next to the jump box to act as a "safety spotter." This encourages careful jumps and helps those students afraid to jump.*

Challenge:

(1) Student turns sideways and jumps sideways off the jump box.

Challenge #1

(2) Student runs up and jumps off the jump box.

NOTE: *Running and jumping is lots of fun and a fast-moving activity. Students need to be warned about running or jumping before the landing area is clear of students.*

BALL AND HOOPS

Promotes: Eye/hand coordination, spatial awareness, directionality.

Need: One ball and five hoops or tires.

Activity:

(1) Hoops are placed in a line on the floor. Student walks to each hoop and bounces and catches ball one time in each hoop. Emphasize control, little bounces.

(2) Student takes ball and rolls it all around the hoop with hands, crawling on knees.

(3) Student rolls ball around hoop controlling it with feet.

Challenge:

(1) Student dribbles the ball, up to five times, outside of the hoop. A hoop is a very confining area in which to learn to control a dribble! Encourage the student to dribble the ball with the fingertips rather than slapping at the ball using the palm of the hand.

COOPERATIVE GAME

Activity:

Old Mrs. Witch: Students join hands in one big circle. One "witch" is in the center. Students swing hands and chant: "Old Mrs. Witch! Old Mrs. Witch! How many children do you have?" The witch in the center answers with a number (example: "five"). The children stamp their feet and shake their hands and count, "one-two-three-four-five." At five, they all scatter and run until the "witch" catches one and that student is the new "witch." The game begins again. This game is always a favorite around Halloween. If it is not Halloween time when you play, feel free to change the witch to a cow, a snake or whatever the children choose.

WEEK 7

WARM-UP

Promotes: Directionality, locomotor skill.

Activity:

(1) *One-half turns:* Students jump forward one jump. They jump again in place and land with back turned to teacher. With each jump forward, students will alternately face and turn back to teacher. The turn is made in the air.

(*Hint:* Ask students to point in the direction to which they will be jumping.)

(2) Jump and tap heels: Students stand with legs slightly apart and jump, kicking up heels. Have them try to reach back and tap heels in air with both hands.

One-half Turns

STEPPING STONES

Promotes: Directionality, locomotor skill, motor planning.

Need: Stepping stones, ball.

Activity:

(1) *One-half turns:* Student starts with both feet in first square, then jumps forward making a half-turn to land in the next square. The turn is made while in the air. Continue pattern throughout the rest of the stones. It helps if student bends arms at elbow and points at each jump.

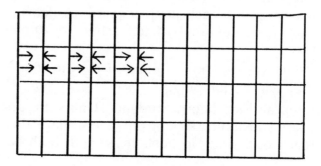

One-half Turns

(2) *Rabbit:* Student places hands and feet in separate squares, jumps hands forward one square and follows with feet. Continue.

Challenge:

(1) Students make up their own pattern using half-turns, and teach to a friend.
(2) Student stands with ball between legs and makes a half-turn jump from square to square.

STUNTS

Promotes: Eye/hand coordination, cooperation, spatial awareness.

Need: Balls.

Activity:

(1) Student bounces the ball, turns around once and catches it. You have to be fast! Younger children will turn and try to hit the ball away because they cannot catch it. Good reaction practice!

(2) Student rolls to a partner *through* the legs of a third person.

(3) Student tosses and catches the ball alone (no higher than head) three to five times.

(4) Student tosses ball, lets it bounce, claps once and catches it.

Activity #2

BALANCE BEAM

Promotes: Dynamic balance, directionality, strengthens arms and shoulders.

Need: Balance beam.

Activity:

(1) *Jumping over the beam:* (a) Stand beside the beam; (b) place hands on beam; (c) jump over beam with arms lifting body. Body will land on other side. Student jumps several times as he or she progresses from one end of the beam to other. (*Hint:* Keep other students clear of beam to avoid getting kicked.)

Challenge:

(1) Student does the above activity with one hand on beam.
(2) Student lays stomach on beam, hands above head on beam. Using hands, student pulls body to end of beam.

Jumping Over the Beam

GAME

Need: Balance beam and two paper cups (one cup half full of water).

Activity:

Balance beam fire drill: Equal number of students wait at each end of beam. First student on each end of beam holds a paper cup. One student holds the cup with water. This student walks across the beam and pours water into the empty cup and then walks back across the beam to the end of the line, after giving the next person in his or her line the now empty cup. Student with water in cup walks across the beam and pours water into empty cup. Repeat until all have had a turn to walk across the beam and pour the water into the empty cup. (Goal: See how much water remains in cup.)

Balance Beam Fire Drill

Variation: Both students with cups could walk to middle of beam and exchange cups of water and walk back to their line and give cup to next person in line.

WEEK 8

WARM-UP

Promotes: Flexibility, strengthens back.

Activity:

(1) *Knee tuck:* Students lie on back, move arms above head, palms down on floor. Bend knees to chest in tuck position. Straighten legs and bend again.

Knee Tuck

(2) *Cobra:* Students lie on stomach, push arms up straight under chest and let head drop back. Bend legs at knees and try to touch head with feet. Point toes! Good for students who may be sway-back.

BALANCE BEAM

Promotes: Eye/foot coordination, spatial awareness, body image.

Need: Balance beam, yardstick, two hoops.

Activity:

(1) Student steps into hoops, then over the crossbar, held by a friend, about six inches off beam.

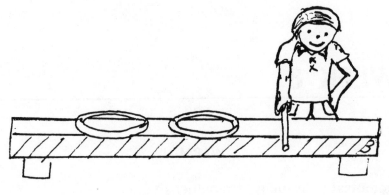

Activity #1

(2) Student walks to middle of beam where a friend is holding the hoop about six inches above the beam. Student steps through the hoop without touching it.

Challenge:

(1) Student performs skill of stepping through the hoop walking backward and sideways.

STEP LAUNCHERS

Promotes: Eye/hand coordination, balance.

Need: Two step launchers, two beanbags.

Activity:

(1) Students step on step launcher and practice getting bags to waist height. Cup hands to catch bag. Remind the student to keep eyes on the beanbag at all times. The harder the student steps on the launcher, the higher and faster it will go!

(2) Student catches bag on back of hands.

Activity #2

(3) Instead of catching the bag, student hits the bag away.

Activity #3

STEPPING STONES

Promotes: Laterality, gross motor coordination.

Need: Stepping stones.

Activity:

(1) *Bunny hop:* With hands and feet each in their own squares, student moves hands one square forward, then feet one square forward. First hands, then feet.

(2) *Monkey:* Student faces sideways with hands and feet each in their own squares. Student moves hands one square sideways, then moves feet one square sideways to line up with hands. Continue.

Challenge:

(1) Students jump sideways from square to square.

(2) Students place each foot in a different square and run through squares. This motion resembles football players working on their warm-up drills. Good coordination is needed to perform this task fast.

COOPERATIVE GAME

Need: One hoop for each eight students.

Activity:

Handy hoop: Players stand in circles of six to eight students. First player drops hoop over head, picks it up and puts it over head of second person. Together they lift it off and drop it over the head of another player. The three of them lift it off and carry it to another player. The activity continues until all students are holding the hoop together. How many hands can you get on a hoop?

WEEK 9

WARM-UP

Promotes: Balance, body image, gross motor coordination.

Activity:

(1) Students stand on one foot, arms out for balance, other foot bent at the knee. Change feet and balance on the other foot. Add a counting exercise to this activity by all counting together or saying the alphabet.

(2) *Step-hop:* Student steps forward on right foot and hops on it. Then student steps on the left foot and hops on it. Work up a rhythm. For classroom practice on this pre-skip activity, a stick "broom" horse or yardstick is a great help. It gives the hands something to do and "divides" the body for further concentration on this step-hop process.

(3) *Wiggle:* Student gets on hands and knees, puts head down looking at stomach and wiggles at waist. Look to the right and wiggle! Look to the left and wiggle!

BALANCE BEAM

Promotes: Static balance, kinesthetic awareness.

Need: Balance beam; hoops.

Activity:

(1) *Stork balance:* Student walks forward to middle of beam and balances on one foot, the other leg bent at the knee and held well off the beam. Achieve balance and count to five. Then continue walking off the beam.

Stork Balance

(2) *Walk over hoops:* Place two hoops on beam, one at each end. Student steps over hoops without touching them, while holding arms folded out in front of body.

STUNTS

Promotes: Directionality, arm strength.

Need: Two scooters and three cones (or chairs or hoops for markers).

Activity:

(1) Student lies on scooter with stomach placed on middle of scooter and pulls self along floor with arms following a path around the markers. Two students may scoot at one time, but not too close to one another.

NOTE: *More parts of the body are being used in a controlled manner when turning or moving around objects. This is the reason for the curvy course.*

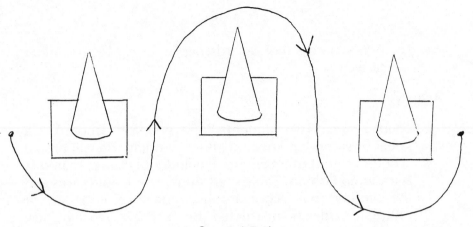

Scooter Path

LADDER

Promotes: Spatial awareness, directionality, gross motor coordination.

Need: Ladder.

Activity:

(1) Teacher and student hold ends of ladder to steady it during this lesson. Place ladder on side (rail) while students creep in and out the windows. Sing: "Go in and out the windows, go in and out the windows, go in and out the windows, as we can go today."

Challenge:

(1) Students creep in and out every other window. This is a body patterning activity. Being able to move in a pattern is a math-related skill giving rise to logical thinking and a greater feel for the understanding of patterns in general.

(2) Students creep backwards through the windows.

GAME

Need: Two scooters, color cards, alphabet cards or number cards.

Activity:

Scoot-a-rama: Two students (one on each scooter) will kneel or sit on left knee. Right leg and left arm will propel scooter around room where remainder of class is seated in a scattered fashion. The seated students will hold cards and the scooters will scoot around certain color, letter, or number cards as instructed by teacher. Teacher may choose letters, vowel sounds, colors or whatever students need to practice. After two turns, teacher chooses two new scooters until each student has a chance to scoot.

NOTE: *This activity can also be used successfully on the stepping stones and ladder by taping the colors or letters to the square so the students can hop or jump to the correct answer.*

Scoot-a-Rama

WEEK 10

WARM-UP

Promotes: Kinesthetic awareness, spatial awareness, directionality.

Activity:

(1) *Slow-motion jumping jacks:* First practice arm movement, then feet, and then put the two together. Emphasize slow, controlled movement.

(2) *One-quarter turns in the air:* Students jump and turn 90 degrees each time until student has jumped four times and returned to the front. Point fingers in the correct direction. (*Hint:* The teacher can help the students locate the side to which they are to jump by calling out, "Jump and face the book case; jump and face the door; jump and face the window; jump and face me. That took four jumps to go around. Let's try it again.")

(3) Students jump and make a quarter-turn in opposite direction.

STUNTS

Promotes: Arm strength, leg strength, directionality.

Need: Two scooters and three cones (or chairs for markers).

Activity:

(1) Student sits on scooter, feet crossed, and moves scooter around cones with hands.

(2) Student goes backward around cones. Going backward is difficult so a friend may have to direct student around markers.

(3) Student lies on back and pushes scooter around cones with legs.

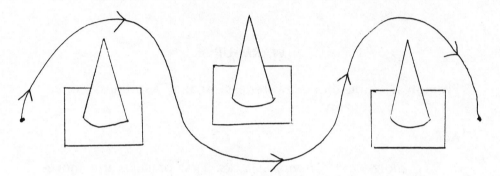

Scooter Path

JUMP BOX

Promotes: Directionality, self-confidence, kinesthetic awareness.

Need: Jump box, hoop placed on mat, or grass or rug at end for safety.

Activity:

(1) Student walks up incline board onto jump box and takes proper jumping position. Student releases with both feet at once and jumps into hoop. Hands are not used in landings. Maintain balance. Remind student to look straight ahead.

Challenge:

(1) Student jumps off jump box making a quarter-turn in the air.

(2) Student jumps off jump box making a half-turn in the air.

NOTE: *It is imperative to keep a spotter on duty! The head has a tendency to fall forward so students will want to jump far from box.*

LADDER

Promotes: Laterality, gross motor coordination.

Need: Ladder.

Activity:

> (1) Student jumps between rungs to end of ladder and *returns* doing a four-legged walk with hands and feet *on* rungs. Let students decide whether this will be a bear walk or a crab walk.

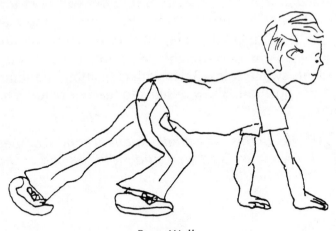

Bear Walk

Challenge:

> (1) Student jumps with one foot outside rail and one foot inside the rail.

Crab Walk

CREATIVE COOPERATIVE MOVEMENT

Activity:

The sculptor and the clay: Two students will work together, one student as the sculptor, the other as the clay. The sculptor will place the clay in various body designs.

Example: Arm out straight, leg bent, twisted, etc. Then students switch roles. Begin with clay sitting, standing, or in a prone position. Show designs to teacher before changing roles.

NOTE: *Keep this beautiful experience noncompetitive! Everyone wins when a student thinks and creates for himself/herself.*

Sculptor   *Clay*

WEEK 11

CREATIVE DRAMATICS DAY

Need: One sheet of newspaper for each student to hold.

NOTE: *Because Week 11 usually occurs during December, a different format is offered as an outlet for that "Holiday Spirit" students are feeling. Three creative activities, each 20 minutes in duration, are suggested. The teacher may choose whichever ones seem to fit the class mood.*

Activity:

(1) *Snowstorm:* Students find space to lie down and teacher tells the story. Students use newspaper in a variety of ways suggested by the italicized words. "You are in bed with your *blanket.* It is very cold tonight. Go to sleep and in the morning there will be a surprise for you to see. Ding! There is the alarm! Wake up! Put on your *bathrobe,* and walk down to the bathroom. Wash your face with the *wash cloth* and dry it with the *towel.* Brush your teeth! Now, pull on your jeans and *shirt* and go downstairs to breakfast. Eat your cereal, drink your juice. Don't forget to put your *napkin* in your lap! Now, let's finish our toast and clean our faces with our *napkins.* Let's go outside and see what has been happening. Pull on your boots, put on your *coat,* don't forget your hat, scarf, and mittens. Open the door and look around! What has happened? It is snowing!"

(Teacher starts to tear off little pieces of paper from her sheet and toss them in the air.) "Make some *snow.* And you know what you do with snow, don't you? You make a *snowball,* and toss it to somebody!"

All students tear up paper and toss it around in a snowball fight. After the storm, students "shovel" all those tiny snowflakes back into the trash can.

75

(2) *Keep in touch:* The experience begins with students walking alone or with a partner, locking elbows, not touching anyone else but the partner. This is the high level of movement. At teacher's signal, students move to middle level (a lower position of the student's choice: sitting, kneeling, etc.). Lastly, students try to keep in touch (elbow to elbow perhaps) at the lowest level possible. Students can move side to side, circle, sway, move backwards or twist at the various levels.

Challenge students to move from one side of the room to the other at high, then middle and then low levels. This time partners connect with two others to make four in a group. The foursome moves across the floor while keeping in touch constantly. Stress slow movement. Students can experiment touching elbow, one finger, head, or hand so long as they touch at least one person in the group at all times.

(3) *First dance:* Lesson begins with students walking around room without touching anyone. The teacher claps her hands to a walking rhythm while students continue walking for one minute—walk to all corners of room. Then students stop and sit in place. Teacher explains different levels of movement: High is standing up, middle is sitting on floor and low is lying on the floor. Practice with students: "Show me your low level, high level, middle level." Repeat. "Move where you are at middle level—use whole body, neck, elbows, spine. Using one movement (making circles in air, turning, rocking, moving arms) go from a high level to a middle level to a low level. Now use three different movements to go from a high to middle then to a low level." Repeat each movement three times at each level before changing levels. Reverse directions and try going low to middle to high. The students have composed their first dance!

Variations: (1) After the students have practiced their dance, half of the students may show the rest of the class their dance. (2) For younger students, the teacher may make up movements and lead the class in dance as they move from level to level together.

High Level

Middle Level

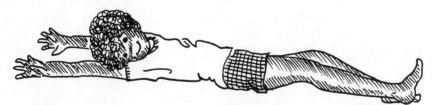

Low Level

WEEK 12

WARM-UP

Promotes: Gross motor coordination, spatial awareness, creative thinking.

Activity:

(1) *Windmill:* Using whole arm, students make big circles in front of the body while in a standing position. Using legs, students make big circles in air while lying down.

(2) Students lie on side and make small circles in the air with leg.

(3) *Running in place:* Students run softly, loudly, lightly, heavily, quickly and slowly. Run through mud (squish, squish), through glue (pull, pull), through hot sand (ouch, ouch) and through a field of flowers (tiptoe, tiptoe). Perform movement while saying words.

LADDER

Promotes: Locomotor control, motor planning.

Need: Ladder.

Activity:

(1) *Bunny hop:* Student does bunny hop between and over rungs of ladder. They first move hands to rung, then jump feet to next space.

(2) Student places both feet inside first set of rungs. Student jumps feet out of rungs to outside of ladder rails, then back to inside next space. Continue the pattern to the end of the ladder.

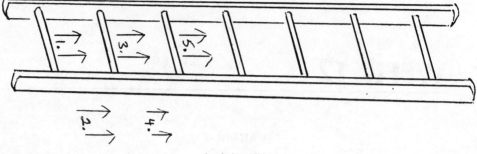

Activity #2

Challenge:

(1) *Double jump* inside rungs of ladder, and then jump both feet out to outsides of ladder rails. Rhythm: In, in, out . . . in, in, out . . . etc. (*Hint:* Students can straddle ladder for "out, out" part of the activity. Another student jumps to side as in activity #2.)

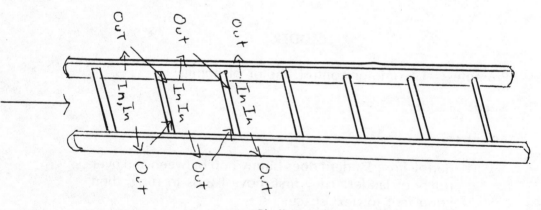

Challenge #1

STUNTS

Promotes: Arm strength, directionality, gross motor coordination.

Need: Two scooters and three cones.

Activity:

(1) Student sits on scooter cross-legged and uses both arms to propel self around cones.

(2) Student makes three or more continuous circles around the cone.

(3) Students play "follow the leader."

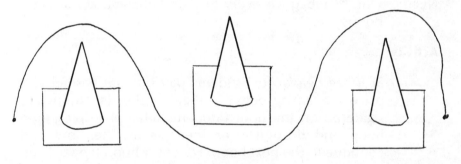

Scooter Path

JUMP BOX

Promotes: Kinesthetic awareness, tactile awareness, self-esteem.

Need: Jump box, tape on floor about 18 to 24 inches past jump box.

Activity:

(1) Student crawls up incline board to jump box, takes proper jumping position with feet apart, releases with both feet at the same time and jumps *onto* the taped line. Each student should take at least three jumps. (*Remember:* Students are to land on balls of feet with knees slightly bent.)

Challenge:

(1) Student walks up sideways and jumps off sideways, landing straddling the taped line.

(2) Student walks up sideways and jumps off sideways while clapping hands and landing *past* the taped line. (*Hint:* Spot all students carefully here. Because the head is still the heaviest part of the body, it tends to come forward on a jump and could get close to the edge of the box when jumping.)

COOPERATIVE GAME

Need: One beanbag for every two students and about eight hoops.

Activity:

(1) *Beanbag headache:* Students pair off with partner and place a beanbag between their foreheads. Hoops are scattered on the floor. Students attempt to pick up a hoop and drop it over their heads, step out and continue to the next hoop. For every hoop they pick up and drop, they collectively score a point. Lots of cooperation is needed in game.

Variation: Each student places beanbag between knees and jumps around attempting to jump into the hoop and lift it over head to get out before progressing to another hoop.

UNILATERAL MOVEMENTS

Using one side of the body at a time

The word unilateral means one-sided. In this phase of the program we are bringing students to an awareness that they have two very useful sides of their bodies: A right and a left. We will be isolating one side of the body in most activities. In addition, we will be naming that side as often as possible—"left" and "right." A hop uses only one side of the body, a slide directs you to right or left, a gallop uses one leg to lead. These are all appropriate movements to bring out an awareness of each side of the body.

In our world, laterality is a very important concept, appearing in reading, writing, numeration, driving, and eating, to name only a few activities. It is important to focus students' attention on their left and right and to create an early awareness of this essential concept.

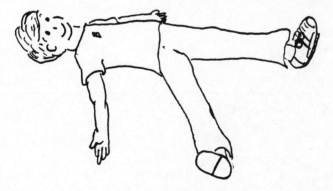

Half an Angel

WEEK 13

WARM-UP

Promotes: Balance, spatial awareness.

Activity:

(1) Students raise left foot, achieve balance, and count to ten. Repeat on right foot. Emphasis: Keep foot on floor motionless. Close eyes and repeat.

(2) Students balance on two body parts (example: one foot, one hand), on three body parts (example: foot, hand, head), on four body parts and on five body parts.

(3) *Finding space:* Directional approach: Walk, hop, and jump in all directions, saying "left" and "right" when appropriate.

STEPPING STONES

Promotes: Laterality, locomotor skills, motor planning.

Need: Stepping stones.

Activity:

(1) Students gallop through squares, always keeping one foot in front.

(2) Students place both hands on right leg and gallop through squares.

Challenge:

(1) Students hop in a zigzag pattern through squares.

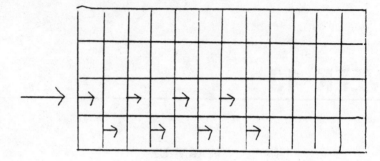

Challenge #1

(2) Students hop, jump or take large steps backwards in a zigzag pattern.

BALANCE BEAM

Promotes: Laterality, dynamic balance, fun!

Need: Balance beam.

Activity:

(1) Student faces the side and slides to the right, saying "right" each time the right foot moves. This continues to end of beam.

(2) Student faces side of beam and slides to left, saying "left" each time the left foot moves. This continues to end of beam.

(3) Student repeats slide to right with military salute using right hand, saying "right" each time right foot moves.

STUNTS

Promotes: Laterality, motor planning, gross motor coordination.

Need: Mats, rug or grass.

Activity:

(1) *Unilateral crawl:* One-sided crawl is another name. Student gets in crawling position and crawls, moving right arm and right leg forward at the *same* time, and left leg and left arm at the *same* time. (*Hint:* The teacher can help by standing over the student, rocking his or her body back and forth and forward—or by holding an arm and leg and moving them together to let student *feel* the sensation of a unilateral crawl. It is a difficult but satisfying movement to create.)

(2) Student unilateral crawls backward and sideways.

Challenge:

(1) *Three-legged crawl dragging right foot:* Student crawls in natural manner, but with right leg extended behind the body.

Three-legged Crawl

COOPERATIVE GAME

Activity:

(1) *Do as I do plus:* Students form two small circles. First student performs one stunt (example: hop on one foot). Second student repeats movement and adds one of own. Third student repeats first two and adds one of own. Encourage students to give helping hints if a stunt is forgotten or not easily recalled. This game teaches students to be more helpful to each other, in addition to strengthening memory and sequencing skills.

Variation: If students desire, one student can create two poses and see if class can duplicate them in proper sequence. Try adding three poses and see how many the class can remember (example of poses are the stork stand, squat position, crawl position, etc.).

WEEK 14

WARM-UP

Promotes: Visual pursuit, develop concept of fixation.

Activity:

(1) Teacher sits in front of class. The students follow her hand movements using only their eyes. The teacher uses the index finger and moves it very slowly in a straight line, up and down in a large zigzag pattern, and diagonally. Remind students to keep their heads still. It is time for the eyes to work. Always work from students' left to right.

(2) Students perform above activity by covering one eye, then the other.

(3) Students turn to partner and perform activity #1 with partners. Remind students this is helpful only if performed slowly and steadily. Use rotary direction, vertical and horizontal. It is important to exercise the muscles of the eyes in a left to right pattern.

BALANCE BEAM

Promotes: Awareness of right and left, dynamic balance.

Need: Balance beam.

Activity:

(1) Slide with hands on knees: Student steps up on beam, faces the side and steps to the right, sliding left foot up to the right. Keep hands on knees while sliding!

(2) Student places right hand on hip and left arm over head, bends body at waist to right and slides to the right.

(3) Student places left hand on hip and right arm over head, bends body at waist to left and slides to the left.

Activity #3

LADDER

Promotes: Tactility, directionality, cooperation.

Need: Ladder; ball, yarn ball or balloon.

Activity:

(1) Student and teacher hold ladder on side (rails) to steady it. Student crawls *on side* in and out the windows of ladder. (*Hint:* This activity is similar to the side stroke in water. Ask your students if they can swim on their sides.)

(2) Student crawls in and out the windows of ladder pushing the ball in front of self. This calls for great control of ball, with small gentle pushes! A yarn ball or balloon may be needed until more control is acquired.

(3) *Follow the leader:* Two students crawl in and out of ladder, the first crawling backward, the second forward. Watch out for your partner's feet!

STUNTS

Promotes: Spatial awareness, gross motor coordination.

Need: Two hoops and two balls.

Activity:

(1) Student crawls around outside of hoop while rolling ball on inside of hoop with fingertips. This strengthens finger muscles for writing skills.

(2) Student crawls around outside of hoop, rolling ball inside of hoop with head, elbow, leg, nose, etc.

Challenge:

(1) Student walks around hoop, ball between ankles, controlling ball with feet. Remind students that controlling a ball with other parts of the body is a soccer skill!

GAME

Activity:

(1) *My point:* Teacher begins as leader. A student may take a turn giving directions as game progresses.

"Touch your nose to the floor, ear to floor, head to floor, elbow to floor, shoulder to floor, wrist to floor, knuckles to floor, and bottom *on* the floor! Now we are going to begin to use our hands and point. Point to your front, your back, your sides. Point up, down, and in front of you. Place your hand *under* your chin, between your knees, above your ears, behind your back, beside your nose. Point to your left arm, right arm, left foot, right foot. Point to the bottom of your feet, place hands inside shoes or pockets."

To end the exercise, have students point to the front, back, sides, etc., of some object outside themselves; for example, a chair, hoop, the room itself, or another student.

WEEK 15

Promotes: Body image, laterality.

Activity:

(1) *Simon says:* "Students, put right hand on right hip, right hand on right ear, right hand on right leg, etc. Place right ear on floor, right elbow on floor, right knee on floor, etc." Then work on the left side of the body. Younger students can practice touching and naming different parts of their bodies.

(2) *Elephant walk:* Student leans left hand on left knee and right hand on right knee and walks forward.

Variation: Students may want to use arms for elephant's trunk. They bend over, clasp hands together and swing arms side to side. They walk slowly and heavily like an elephant.

(3) *Kick:* Students extend right hand to front of body and kick with right foot. Repeat with left hand and foot.

BALANCE BEAM

Promotes: Cooperation, dynamic balance.

Need: Balance beam, tiny bell, tiny basket full of beads or beans, any interesting item.

Activity:

(1) Student walks across beam carrying bell, trying *not* to ring it. Lots of body control is needed.

(2) Student walks across beam carrying tiny basket full of beads. If beads fall, lots of cooperation is needed from friends to help pick up!

Challenge:

(1) Student stands facing the side on the balance beam— placing feet shoulder-width apart, feet turned outward, toes pointing to ends of the beam. Student bends knees while keeping toes turned outward, then straightens up and takes two steps. Then student bends, straightens and steps again. This continues until student reaches end of beam.

Challenge #1

(2) Student stands in position described in #1 and slides to the right while keeping toes pointed outward toward end of beam.

STUNTS

Promotes: Locomotor skill, spatial awareness.

Need: Rope, yarn, string, etc.

Activity:

(1) Teacher and one student hold ends of rope and adjust the height to suit the activity. Teacher instructs students to leap over, crawl under, jump over, step over, crawl over, drag body under rope.

(2) Student repeats above movements backward and sideways.

(3) Two ropes held by student and teacher may be also used in an "X" design for activity #1. Ask the students to recite their actions: crawling "over," crawling "under," etc.

Challenge:

(1) *Jump to height of rope:* Two students hold up ends of rope about three inches over heads of remaining students. Students jump and try to touch head to rope. Positions are changed and activity continues until all have had a chance to hold the rope and jump.

STEPPING STONES

Promotes: Motor planning, laterality.

Need: Stepping stones.

Activity:

(1) *Drop back:* Student hops (or jumps if necessary) three squares forward and then hops backward two squares. Repeat pattern to end of stones.

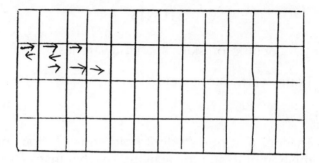

Drop Back

(2) *Gorilla walk:* Student places both feet in one square, leans left hand on left knee and right hand on right knee and walks heavily through the squares forward and then backward.

COOPERATIVE GAME

Activity:

One little elephant: Song: One little el-e-phant went out to play! Out on a spi-der's web one day! He had such e-nor-mous fun, he called for another lit-tle elephant to come! Two little el-e-phants went out to play! etc. . . .

Game: One (student) elephant walks (like an elephant, bent at waist and arms clasped for trunk) in a circle around a web (hula hoop) in front of class. When class says, "He called for another little elephant," the student chooses another friend to walk along. The game continues until everyone has been chosen and all the elephants are walking in a circle around the web.

WEEK 16

Promotes: Awareness of left and right, body image.

Activity:

(1) *Half an angel:* Student lies on floor, slides right leg and right arm along floor to half-angel position, then returns. The activity is repeated on left side. Teacher can call, "Right—left—right," and see how students respond.

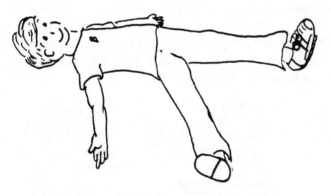

Half an Angel

(2) Students lie on floor and draw a circle in the air with right foot, a triangle in the air with left foot and a square in the air with right arm and right foot.

LADDER

Promotes: Eye/hand coordination, dynamic balance.

Need: Ladder and ball.

Activity:

(1) Student walks on outside of ladder and bounces and catches a ball in spaces *between* ladder rungs.

(2) Student walks with one foot on each of the ladder rails, bounces and catches ball between rungs. Younger students may stand between rungs and roll or push the ball in front of them. Emphasize small, controlled bounces.

BALANCE BEAM

Promotes: Balance, awareness of left and right, cooperation.

Need: Balance beam.

Activity:

(1) *Right, right, right:* Two students join hands and stand facing sideways on beam. They slide to right three steps, stop, drop hands, and clap or shake right hands together three times, saying, "right, right, right." They continue pattern to end.

Right, Right, Right

(2) Students repeat above activity to left, clapping or shaking left hands together, saying "left, left, left."

BALLOON VOLLEYBALL

Promotes: Eye/hand coordination, cooperation.

Need: One balloon, string.

Activity:

(1) Balloon is suspended from string, held at ends by two students. Two other students bat balloon back and forth across string with right hand, then with left hand.

NOTE: *Teacher's comments here can reinforce concepts of right and left: "That was a great left-hand hit," or "Gee, is your right hand strong!"*

(2) Students kick balloon with right foot, then left foot. Stress taking turns!

Activity #1

COOPERATIVE GAME

Activity:

Eye to eye: Students choose a partner and stand facing partner folding arms in front of self. Student stands and touches partner's folded arms, elbow to elbow. They walk around keeping elbows touching, then jump around room, elbows still touching. The students have to decide how to move and when to jump in order to keep together.

Variation: Students face partner, placing hands on each other's shoulders (or palm to palm), keeping back straight and head high. They move with stiff, straight legs.

Eye to Eye

WEEK 17

Promotes: Laterality, creativity.

Activity:

(1) *Wicket walk:* Students bend forward and grasp the legs just above the ankle. Without releasing the grip, students take a short step with the right foot, then step with the left. They continue forward and try sideways and backwards.

(2) *Washing machine game:* In this creative dramatics activity, each student imagines he or she is a piece of clothing. "First, we jump into the washing machine and we are washed, sloshing around. Next, we are in the dry cycle, spinning around and being wrung out. We are hung out to dry on the clothes line, dripping wet. We are blowing in the wind; we are taken off the line, folded, placed side by side, and carried up the stairs and put away in a dresser drawer."

NOTE: *For safety's sake, be sure to remind students that nothing goes in the washing machine at home except real clothes.*

BALANCE BEAM

Promotes: Laterality, dynamic balance, tactility.

Need: Balance beam.

Activity:

(1) Student walks across beam dipping first one foot, then taking a step on it, then dipping the other and stepping on it. To dip, leg on beam bends slightly and other foot swings along side of the beam. Students love to sing, "*row,* row, *row* your boat," dipping on each accented word.

(2) Student walks along beam performing double dips on each side.

(3) Student places feet sideways on beam, back to floor and hands on floor and crab walks along beam.

Activity #1

Challenge:

(1) Student will dance "La Raspa" on balance beam while in crab walk position. Student touches right foot to beam, then jumps and changes to left foot. Jump and change again.

Challenge #1

LADDER

Promotes: Dynamic balance, gross motor coordination.

Need: Ladder.

Activity:

(1) Student places hands on rungs, back to floor and feet on rungs to perform crab walk along ladder.

(2) *Lame dog walk:* Student places two hands and one foot on rungs to perform lame dog walk along ladder. See if students can tell *why* a lame dog would walk this way! Perhaps the dog has a hurt *front* paw—can students walk like that?

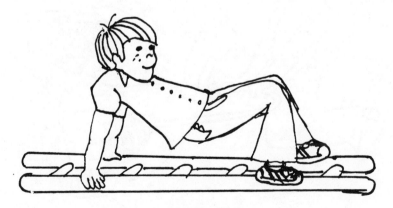

Activity #1

JUMP BOX

Promotes: Gross motor coordination, self-confidence, laterality.

Need: Jump box, hoop or bicycle tire.

Activity:

(1) Student crawls up incline board, stands, jumps and lands with left foot in a tire and right foot outside the tire placed slightly to left of jump box. On second jump, student can land with right foot in one tire, and left foot outside the tire. (*Hint:* A large part of the student's weight is on the leg and ankle when the student is jumping to land with one foot in a tire. Landing lightly and carefully is a must.)

(2) Student jumps and lands in a hoop held by students approximately six inches off floor close to edge of box. *Important:* Hold hoop very still so student can jump safely.

Activity #2

COOPERATIVE GAME

Need: One hoop per student.

Activity:

Bears on the move: Each student pretends to be a bear sitting in cave (the hoop) while teacher explains that he or she will help them get comfortable. Teacher says: "Put an arm and a foot on the edge of the cave; now add an elbow. Now, this cave isn't very comfortable! *Bears on the move!*" At this signal, all bears crawl to another cave and teacher begins with another set of body parts to help them get comfortable; for example, one ear, two fingers and one knee in cave. Finally, after trying out several caves, bears find a good cave and go to sleep.

WEEK 18

Promotes: Creative thinking, gross motor coordination.

Activity:

(1) Students make this shape with body: "W." Arms may be used in kneeling position, as one good way to form this letter. Students act out the following words: wiggle, walk, wobble, wince, whirl, whoosh, wind.

Activity #1

(2) *Knee-drop staccato:* Students drop to kneedrop position, one leg bent, other knee on floor as teacher calls, "right knee, left knee." Look for quick, agile reactions. Arms may be out for balance, and students may want to take a little jump between positions to help change legs smoothly. Stress safety to students so they won't bang knee on floor while changing knees!

BALANCE BEAM

Promotes: Cooperation, dynamic balance.

Need: Balance beam, beanbag.

Activity:

(1) *Partner knee drops:* Two students face each other on beam, holding hands. While walking across beam, they perform a knee drop, with one knee bent and resting on beam. They return to standing position, take two steps and repeat, "walk, walk, kneel, stand, etc." They try for a total of three knee drops. Holding hands steadies many students and develops cooperation but if it hampers this activity, students may want to perform together without holding hands—maybe chanting together, "walk, walk, kneel, stand."

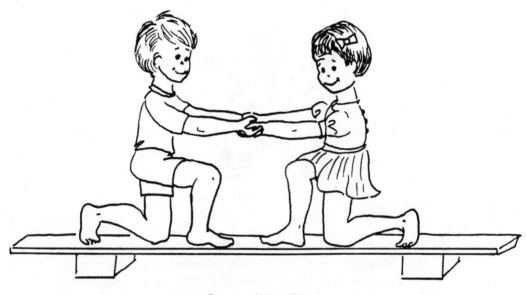

Partner Knee Drops

(2) Two students stand on beam facing each other, holding ends of a ruler and balancing a beanbag on it. They walk forward and backward, balancing carefully to keep that beanbag from falling.

JUMP BOX

Promotes: Cooperation, self-confidence, fun!

Need: Jump box, two hoops.

Activity:

(1) Hoops are placed side by side in front of the jump box. Student jumps and claps while landing in left hoop.

(2) Student jumps and claps while landing in right hoop.

(3) Two students jump and call direction of hoop they will land in: "right" or "left."

(4) Student jumps and calls own *full* name: "Mary Jane Smith."

STEPPING STONES

Promotes: Cooperation, laterality.

Need: Stepping stones, ball.

Activity:

(1) *Ball drop:* Student steps through center lane of stones stopping at each square to drop and catch ball in two squares located in front to the right and to the left of student.

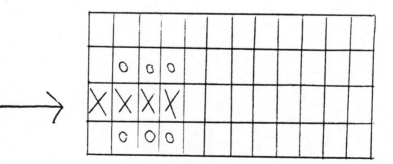

Ball Drop

(2) Two students roll ball back and forth slowly to each other across the stepping stones as they step sideways through the stones. If the students have the skills they can play catch while sliding through stepping stones. They may also count the number of rolls or steps necessary to complete this activity.

Challenge:

(1) Students jump from square to square with ball between their ankles.

(2) Students sit on floor in front of stepping stones with arms in back supporting body and place ball between knees, using hands and feet to move from square to square.

COOPERATIVE GAME

Need: One ball for every ten students.

Activity:

Hands off: Divide class into two groups of students, ten each. Students sit in circle. One student gently kicks the ball with the bottom of feet. While sitting, students keep the ball in motion using only their feet. If the ball is kicked out of the circle, it is retrieved using the feet only!

Variation: Count the kicks. See how many times players can kick without the ball leaving the circle. When it is kicked out, begin counting over.

WEEK 19

Promotes: Cooperation, leg and arm strength, creative thinking.

Activity:

(1) *Rowboat:* Students sit facing partner, holding hands and feet in contact, legs extended. One student leans forward and the other student leans back.

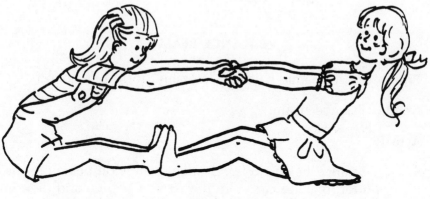

Rowboat

(2) Students get out of boat and pretend to play catch with various sizes of balls. "Toss" a beach ball, baseball, bowling ball and balloon. "Pop" balloon and blow up another.

STEP LAUNCHER

Promotes: Tactility, laterality, eye/hand coordination.

Need: Two step launchers and two beanbags.

Activity:

(1) Student steps on step launcher with left foot and catches beanbag with left hand, shoulder, elbow, etc. This takes a controlled, careful stomp!

(2) Student steps on step launcher with right foot and catches beanbag with right hand, shoulder, elbow, etc.

(3) Student steps on step launcher with preferred foot and launches bag over head. Student must duck to let bag pass over head. This takes a strong stomp and quick reactions. It is lots of fun and requires a good deal of free area to let the bag fly. "Blast off!" is an appropriate yell as the bag flies up and over the student's head.

BALANCE BEAM

Promotes: Dynamic balance, laterality, form perception.

Need: Balance beam.

Activity:

(1) *Balance beam circles:* Student stands on beam on one foot, making circles in the air first behind and then in front of body with other foot. Arms are out for balance; legs are alternated. Student takes two steps forward and makes a total of three sets of circles, continuing to end of beam.

(2) *Half-turns:* Student steps up on beam facing left side. Student slides one step to right, makes a half-turn (180 degrees), slides one step to left, makes a half-turn and continues to end of beam.

Half Turns

STEPPING STONES

Promotes: Motor planning, laterality.

Need: Stepping stones.

Activity:

(1) *March:* Student marches through stones slapping right knee with right hand and left knee with left hand, calling, "right, left," as each step is taken.

(2) Student begins standing in first square on left. Student hops sideways saying, "right, right, right." Then he or she hops two squares forward and hops to the left saying, "left, left, left." Pattern continues to end of stones.

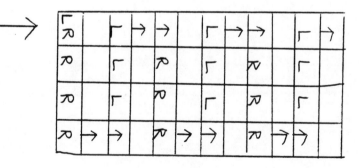

Activity #2

COOPERATIVE GAME

Activity:

Nests: Students scatter around the room, running on tiptoes. On the signal "nests," they find one partner, join hands and twirl in a circle "building a nest" for a bird. On the signal "fly," they move together around the room until the signal "nests" is given again. This time, they join another couple and twirl in a circle. The game continues until one large nest is built with all children joined together.

WEEK 20

Promotes: Overall body tone, creativity.

Activity:

(1) Students stand tall, reach for the ceiling and really s - t - r - e - t - c - h! Pantomime picking apples stretching up high, first with the left arm, and then with the right arm.

(2) Students sit with legs in open position. Students stretch right hand to left ankle and then left hand to right ankle. Head to knee *if they can!* Please don't strain!

(3) *Creative dramatics:* Students show with creative movements how these kitchen appliances move: blender, toaster, coffee pot, hand mixer, can opener, whistling kettle. (*Hint:* "Show me your blender; how would you move if you were a toaster; etc.")

STUNTS

Promotes: Leg strength, abdominal strength, cooperation.

Need: Mats, soft surface.

Activity:

(1) *Inchworm:* Students assume push-up position and walk legs up to hands, then hands walk forward to a slanting position, keeping legs straight. Keep those hands flat!

Inchworm

(2) *Tired toes:* Students lie on back, touching head to head with a partner. Students hold partner's hands, arms remaining on floor. Both students lift legs straight up into the air then lower to right and to left. Stress keeping legs closed and hands held tight.

Tired Toes

LADDER

Promotes: Gross motor coordination, spatial awareness, directionality.

Need: Ladder placed in an incline position using chair, jump box, etc.

Activity:

(1) Students crawl up ladder on hands and knees.

(2) Students do four-legged bear walk up ladder, using hands and feet on rungs.

Challenge:

(1) Students walk forward up rungs to end and jump off.

(2) Students walk down rungs of ladder, arms out for balance. Some students will require a spotter or a hand to hold to steady them.

STEPPING STONES

Promotes: Motor planning, cooperation.

Need: Stepping stones.

Activity:

(1) *Triple hop:* Student begins on right foot and hops three squares, changes to left foot and hops three squares and changes to right for three more, then three on left to finish.

(2) Students hold hands with a partner and hop as described in activity #1.

(3) Students count out loud, "one, two, three; one, two, three," as they hop on each foot. Older students enjoy spelling three letter words as they hop, "C - A - T, D - O - G, H - O - P, R - U - N, etc." If they are working on any consonant or vowel sounds they may repeat them out loud.

COOPERATIVE GAME

Activity:

(1) *Triple back:* Students stand back to back in groups of three and walk around the room without letting go of each other.

(2) *"Six little ducks"* (Action Song): Students use whole body to act out this song.

"Six little ducks that I once knew,
Fat ones, skinny ones and tall ones too.
But the one little duck with the feathers on his back,
He led the others with a quack, quack, quack!
Quack, quack, quack; quack, quack, quack,
He led the others with a quack, quack, quack!
Down to the river they would go,
Wibble, wobble, wibble, wobble, to and fro,
But the one little duck with the feathers on his back,
He led the others with his quack, quack, quack!"

WEEK 21

Promotes: Creativity, fun!

Activity: *The firefighter:* Each firefighter is asleep, and then the alarm rings. Firefighters dress, putting on boots and pants, slide down the pole, jump on the fire truck and drive, turning left and right. They rush to the fire, unload a hose and attach it to a fire hydrant. They climb the ladder with the hose on their backs, spray water on the fire and then climb down. They spot someone trapped in the building and form a circle holding hands to catch the jumping fire victim. They put out the rest of the fire, shovel out the burned area and then board the fire engine to return to the station and back to sleep. (*Hint:* Be sure to allow plenty of leeway for deviations to the basic story. Every child has an idea of what a firefighter should do and we don't want to disappoint anybody!)

STEPPING STONES

Promotes: Motor planning, awareness of right and left.

Need: Stepping stones.

Activity:

(1) *Jump, jump, tap, tap:* Students place hands on hips and jump forward two squares, stop and tap on the right with the right foot and on the left with the left foot. Continue pattern to end of stepping stones. (*Hint:* There are endless variations to this activity. Try pointing with arm as toe taps or add a nod of the head or a clap. Some students like to jump forward two steps and then jump to each side and back to the center.)

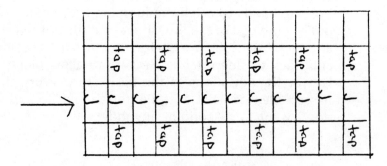

Jump, Jump, Tap, Tap

(2) *Step-hop:* Students alternately step and hop through the stepping stones. This is fun for those who love hop-scotch and a lead-up activity to skipping.

BALANCE BEAM

Promotes: Laterality, dynamic balance.

Need: Balance beam.

Activity:

(1) *Half-angel:* Student steps on left foot and raises right arm and leg out to side. Then student steps on right foot and raises left arm and leg out to side. This pattern continues to end of beam.

Half Angel

(2) Student performs four-legged walk with both arms and both feet on beam. This is difficult but good for muscle control.

Activity #2

Challenge:

(1) *Monkey:* Student places hands on beam, feet on ground in a squat position. Arms move to right one jump and then legs follow. This continues to end of beam.

STUNTS

Promotes: Arm strength, cooperation.

Need: Scooter board, rope, traffic cone.

Activity:

(1) *Toe ride:* Students assume push-up position, toes on scooter. They use arms to propel body across floor. Legs are extended *straight* and *toes* ride on scooter.

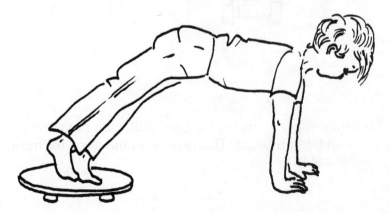

Toe Ride

(2) *Friendly ride:* One student sits on scooter holding end of rope, while second student pulls rope. The rider can request a ride in a *circle, around* a traffic cone, or can direct puller to turn *right* or *left.*

COOPERATIVE GAME

Activity:

Snap trap: Half the students choose a partner and stand face to face, hold hands together up in the air and move *slowly* in a circle. Balance of class are mice, running through traps. When teacher calls "snap," traps gently lower arms trying to catch a mouse. If a mouse is caught, it becomes a member of the trap. When all are caught, the original traps get a turn playing mouse and the original mice become traps.

CROSS-LATERAL MOVEMENTS

Using both sides of the body in opposition, crossing the midline

Cross-lateral means crossing sides of the body. The right side must cross the center line of the body over to the left side or the left side must cross the center line of the body over to the right side. The term is also used to name movements in which sides work in opposition (for example, the right foot and left arm kicking together). A baby's crawl is a natural cross-lateral movement, as is an adult's walk. These movements take a good basic understanding of left and right and a lot of thinking to accomplish. For this reason we recommend that younger students (ages two and three) return to the unilateral lessons for additional practice or substitute activities when necessary. Not every activity in this section is strictly cross-lateral, but a large variety is provided to give students a chance to experience cross-lateral tasks through gross motor activity. Enjoy!

CROSS-LATERAL MOVEMENTS

Using both sides of the body in opposition, crossing the midline

WEEK 22

WARM-UP

Promotes: Cross-pattern awareness, creativity.

Activity:

(1) *Body division:* Students draw a line with finger from middle of forehead down to nose, to chin, to navel, ending where legs split body. Emphasize the fact that we have two sides of our body. On the right side we have a right eye, right ear, right cheek, right arm, etc., and the same for the left. Explain that the next few lessons will require the children to cross that midline, crossing arms, legs, etc. This brief introduction will acquaint students with the principles that will be taught and help them understand the difference in the next set of lessons.

(2) *Touch and cross:* Simon says, "Use your right hand to touch your right knee; now cross your midline and touch your left knee. Great! Touch your right ear; now cross your midline and touch your left ear. Fine! Touch your right ankle, now your left ankle." Continue touching and crossing and then change hands and start with left hand.

(3) *Cross patterns:* Simon says, "Slowly now, put your right hand on your left knee, your right hand on your left ankle, your right hand over your left eye. Nice! Now let's change hands. Put your left hand over your right eye, left hand on right hip, left hand on right calf . . . etc."

(*Hint:* Remember when a teacher is facing the group, most preschoolers will need the teacher to demonstrate with opposite hand.)

STUNTS

Promotes: Leg and back strength, body flexibility.

Need: Mats or soft surface.

Activity:

(1) Students stand tall, hands on hips. Touch right hand to left ankle and straighten up. Then touch left hand to right ankle and straighten up. Work up to a rhythm and practice in sets of five.

(2) Students sit tailor fashion with hands behind head. Bend forward, slightly twist body and touch right elbow to left knee and left elbow to right knee. Repeat ten times.

(3) Students sit on floor, legs extended, hands in back of body on floor. Lift bottom off the floor in crab-walk position and slide right leg to bottom by bending knee. Jump both legs slightly, change and slide left knee to bent position. Keep switching, counting sets of five.

ROPE

Promotes: Cross-pattern awareness, gross motor coordination.

Need: Rope, string, or yarn, etc.

Activity:

(1) *Cross step:* Two students hold ends of rope about three inches off floor. Student places left foot on right side and right foot on left side. Right foot must be in front. Left foot crosses around back of right foot, over and in front to land on the right side of the rope. Right foot comes around back of the left foot to cross over to the left side of the rope again. Continue.

Cross Step

(2) Students stand in a line, hands on each others' shoulders, and walk cross-step together along rope.

(3) Student stands with feet parallel to rope and jumps sideways and forward (or backward) from side to side of rope to end of rope.

BALANCE BEAM

Promotes: Eye/hand coordination, balance, cross-lateral awareness.

Need: Balance beam.

Activity:

(1) *Give me five:* One student stands on each side of the balance beam near beginning, facing third walking student. Third student walks on beam facing other two students. Student on beam steps on left foot, claps his or her hand to student on left, and then steps on right foot and claps his or her left hand with student on right. Students on each side of beam walk backward while student on beam continues to end of beam. (*Hint:* If lots of students are on hand, place half of class on each side of beam, standing still, and walking student will clap each student's hand while walking to end of beam.)

(2) Repeat above activity with student on beam walking *backward* clapping right and left hands of students on each side of beam. Students on side of beam walk forward.

Give Me Five

COOPERATIVE GAME

Activity:

Winding: Half the students sit in a line, arms out straight, holding hands. Other students form a line standing holding hands and follow leader who knits in and out, stepping over hands of seated students. As leader reaches last seated student, leader sits and begins a new line of sitters. When all the students are seated, sitters stand and, holding hands, take a turn moving through.

Variation: Leader changes pattern and winds through every other student.

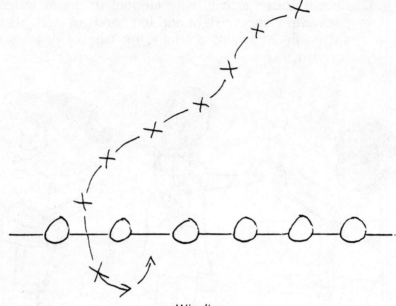

Winding

WEEK 23

WARM-UP

Promotes: Cross-pattern awareness, creativity.

Activity:

(1) *Walking forward strides:* Students place hands on hips and jump one foot forward and one foot back to stride position. Jump and switch. Add arm extensions, hands pointing forward in opposition. Right arm is forward with left foot and left arm with right foot. Develop a rhythm. Try singing a song with this exercise and see if your students can jump to the music.

(2) Students create movement suggested by the following words: A—above, around, angry. B—bend, burrow, break, balloon, balance, backbend. To create large letters, it is fun to choose three students to form the letter with their bodies.

STUNTS

Promotes: Abdominal and back strength, rhythm, cross-pattern awareness.

Need: Mats or soft surface.

Activity:

(1) *Scaling:* Students lie on back, one leg straight in air. Students grasp thigh with both hands and "climb" to the ankle, while sitting up. As students climb down, they lie back down again. This is repeated several times.

Scaling

(2) *Ankle clap:* Students stand straight during exercise. Students lift left leg, right hand clasps ankle, lift right leg, left hand clasps ankle, then three claps in front in combination with three jumps in place, "Ankle, ankle, clap, clap, clap!" Repeat with rhythm.

STEP LAUNCHER

Promotes: Eye/hand coordination, cooperation, cross-pattern awareness.

Need: Two beanbags, two step launchers.

Activity:

(1) Student steps with *left* foot and catches bag with *right* hand, then steps with *right* foot and catches with *left* hand.

(2) One student steps, other student catches bag. Lots of cooperation is required. Students may count off before launching bag or they may have a secret message spoken before take off: "Launch pad clear and ready for takeoff. Count down: ten, nine, eight, etc."

BALANCE BEAM

Promotes: Dynamic balance, gross motor coordination, tactility.

Need: Balance beam, beanbag.

Activity:

(1) Student crawls on beam with beanbag on head, shoulders, back, etc.

(2) Student crawls on beam with eyes closed.

Challenge:

(1) Student walks to end of beam, then backward to middle and performs a knee balance. Arms are out for balance. Student kneels one knee on beam while other knee is bent.

Challenge #1

COOPERATIVE GAME

Activity:

Chorus line: Students stand in one or two long lines, holding hands. They move across room once in each of the following different movement patterns: (a) jump, step; (b) jump, jump, step; (c) step, step, jump, jump; (d) kick left foot to right, kick right foot to left, stomp, stomp, stomp. Say the words while performing the actions.

NOTE: *A pattern in movement is like a mathematical set. A jump, step pattern is an A–B pattern; it has two different elements. Perhaps students can suggest another A–B pattern. The second pattern suggested (jump, jump, step) is a set of movements having three elements, the first two of which are the same:A–A–B. Viewing the movements as a set seems to help some students repeat them with greater accuracy and increases mathematical understanding of sets and patterns in an enjoyable way.*

WEEK 24

Promotes: Gross motor coordination, cross-lateral awareness, cooperation.

Activity:

(1) *Jump and cross:* Students stand tall, feet together and hands on hips. Students jump and cross legs, first right foot in front. Then they jump again and place left foot in front. This is repeated several times. Some students may jump and cross, jump to open stance and then jump and cross again.

(2) *Side by side and face to face:* Partners stand side by side, holding hands. Partners jump and face each other and hold both hands, then jump again to side-by-side position and hold only one hand. They repeat this several times.

Side by Side and Face to Face

139

BALANCE BEAM

Promotes: Gross motor coordination, spatial awareness, arm strength.

Need: Balance beam.

Activity:

   (1) *Straddle:* Student stands with feet straddling beam, hands on beam. Student jumps hands along beam and feet along floor to end of beam.

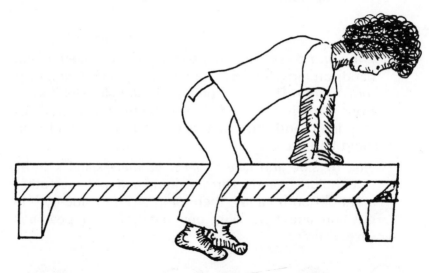

Straddle

   (2) *Straddle jump:* Student stands with feet straddling beam, hands on beam. Student jumps hands along beam while jumping feet alternately on and off beam to end of beam.

   (3) Student lies on back *on beam* bending right knee. Student raises right arm to side and left leg up. Balance and hold. Student repeats with other leg and arm, while bending left knee to maintain balance.

LADDER

Promotes: Dynamic balance, cross-lateral awareness, cooperation.

Need: Ladder, beanbag and one cup of water.

Activity:

(1) *Cross pattern:* Student stands at end of ladder facing side and walks sideways with left foot in front all the way down the ladder between rungs. Left foot stays *crossed over* right.

(2) Student walks forward between rungs or on the rails with a beanbag on right foot and a cup of water in left hand. Student chooses rails or rungs. Students are not crossing the midline but focusing attention on both left *and* right working simultaneously. Lots of thinking is possible here. Students have to decide what moves first and where to focus attention: on the cup of water or on the foot. It is very hard to concentrate on two movements at once. Student may need a friend to help replace the bag if it falls off. Be sure the helper gets lots of praise.

STEPPING STONES

Promotes: Motor planning, gross motor control.

Need: Stepping stones.

Activity:

(1) *Zigzag walk:* Student walks forward crossing right foot over and placing it in the left square. Then left crosses over and steps into the upper right corner square. Continue pattern to end of stepping stones.

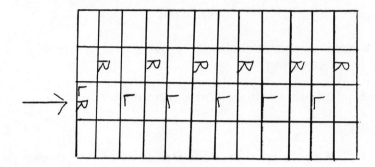

Zigzag Walk

(2) *Side by side and face to face:* Partners each stand in own square side by side on stepping stones, holding hands. They jump one square forward and land face to face holding both hands. They jump forward again and land side by side holding only one hand. They continue to end of stepping stones.

COOPERATIVE GAME

Need: String, yarn, rope.

Activity:

Lower the boom: String is hung between two chairs or two students may hold string. A leader is selected to choose and demonstrate one stunt to be performed while moving under the string. After all students have performed the stunt, lower the string and choose another stunt. Continue to lower string after each stunt. Encourage students not to touch the string. After two stunts, a new leader is chosen. (*Hint:* For shy students, teacher may suggest some stunts: monkey, seal walk, hop, run, skip, snake, etc.)

WEEK 25

WARM-UP

Promotes: Cooperation, flexibility.

Activity:

(1) *Bicycle:* Student lies on back, feet in air, hands on floor. Pedal bicycle, first fast, then slow, high, then low.

(2) *Legs in a basket:* Students choose partners. One student stands; the other lies on back and puts feet in first student's hands. Student on back crosses first one foot, then other foot and touches floor with toes. (*Hint:* If foot does not touch floor, body must twist to help toe reach floor.)

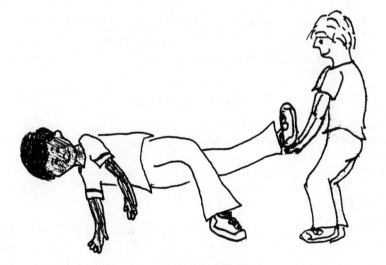

Legs in a Basket

STEPPING STONES

Promotes: Cross-pattern awareness, dynamic balance.

Need: Stepping stones.

Activity:

(1) *Jump and cross:* Student stands with legs crossed. Student jumps forward and crosses legs again to land in next squares. This continues to end of stepping stones. Younger students may jump and cross, jump to open stance and then jump and cross again.

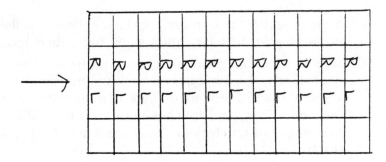

Jump and Cross

(2) Students walk on heels through stepping stones.
(3) Students walk with toes alternately pointed outward and inward, "out, out, in, in."

BALANCE BEAM

Promotes: Cooperation, static balance.

Need: Balance beam.

Activity:

(1) Two students walk to middle from opposite ends of beam and pass each other on beam (walk around), saying, "Excuse me, please." Some students are amazingly adept at this, but there is no problem in one

student putting one foot on the floor and one foot on beam while second student steps over first student's foot and says, "Excuse me, please."

(2) Student gallops by running with one foot in front almost to end of beam and then balances on hands and one knee. Both hands hold beam while one knee is kneeling on beam and other is extended in the air. Student returns to stand and jumps off.

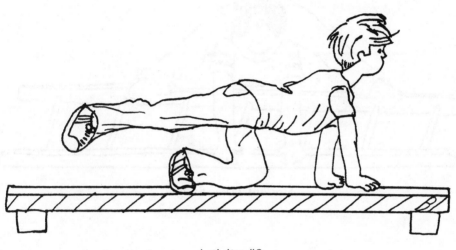

Activity #2

LADDER

Promotes: Coordination, eye/hand coordination, auditory acuity.

Need: Ladder, ping pong ball or rubber ball and tin plate.

Activity:

(1) *Student body bridge:* Student places hands on one rail, feet on other and moves sideways along ladder.

(2) Two students make a bridge over the ladder while another student crawls under bridge.

(3) Student drops table-tennis ball or rubber ball between each rung and catches it with other hand or with a tin plate. Hearing the ball land in the plate is a rewarding experience. Often the other students at this station will spontaneously clap or call, "Yea," each time they hear a "ping."

Student Body Bridge

COOPERATIVE GAME

Need: Balance beam.

Activity:

"Excuse me, please": Three students stand on beam and rest of class stands at end of beam. First student in line walks around A and takes A's place. A moves to B; B moves to C and C joins rest of class. Second student in line walks around A, takes A's place; A moves to B, etc. Continue until all students have a chance to stand on beam. Students standing on beam should remind walking students to say, "Excuse me, please."

Variation: (1) Student places one foot on beam and other foot on floor, which will allow easier passing for student on the beam. (2) Students may walk, hop, or skip a circle around students on beam while saying, "Excuse me, please."

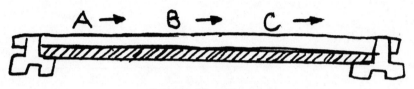

Excuse Me, Please

WEEK 26

Promotes: Flexibility, cross-pattern awareness.

Activity:

(1) *Grapevine:* With feet together, student steps to right on right foot, then crosses left foot over it so that weight is on left foot. Then student steps to side on right foot and crosses left foot *behind* and weight is transferred to left foot. Remember the saying: "Side, over, side, back." Continue.

(2) Student repeats grapevine to left.

(3) *Rocking horse:* Student lies on tummy, bends knees up toward back and then reaches hands back to grasp feet and rocks back and forth.

Rocking Horse

149

BALANCE BEAM

Promotes: Cross-pattern awareness, rhythmic body coordination.

Need: Balance beam.

Activity:

(1) *Grapevine:* Student steps to right on right foot, then crosses left foot over it with weight on left foot. Then steps to side on right foot and crosses left foot behind. Pattern continues across balance beam and back to beginning. Remember the rhythm: side, over, side, back.

(2) *Touch and go (La Raspa):* Four students, two on each side, stand facing beam, holding hands with partner on sides. Students quickly tap alternate feet on beam, working up to a rhythm: Right foot touch, left foot touch. See how fast students can change feet and still maintain balance.

Touch and Go

(3) *Touch and go backward:* Students repeat touch-and-go step with their backs to beam.

STEPPING STONES

Promotes: Cross-pattern awareness, motor planning, gross motor coordination.

Need: Stepping stones, beanbags.

Activity:

(1) *Grapevine:* Student stands with both feet in first square, with side or shoulder facing stones. Student steps to right on right foot, then crosses left foot over it, then steps to right on right foot again and crosses left foot behind. This continues to end of stepping stones. Remember the rhythm: side, over, side, back.

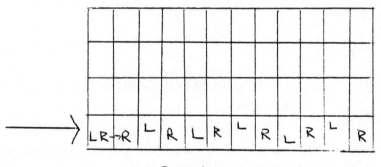

Grapevine

(2) Student throws a beanbag into a square and jumps to it with one jump. Student picks it up and throws it again, then jumps over and past the beanbag. Student throws once with the right hand and then with the left.

LADDER

Promotes: Cooperation, listening skills, motor planning.

Need: Ladder.

Activity:

(1) Student helps another student who is covering his or her eyes to walk, jump and hop through the rungs. First student takes other student's hand and talks that student through the ladder. "Sightless" student waits to be told what to do next.

(2) *Pattern walk:* Student walks a pattern of rungs and rails along ladder.

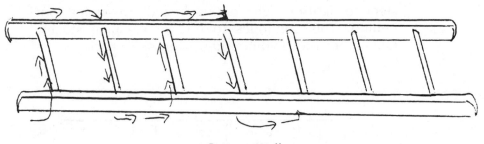

Pattern Walk

COOPERATIVE GAME

Activity:

Student bridges: Students stand in two groups, one group of boys and one group of girls. Girls make bridges in the following ways: backbend bridges; one hand, one foot bridges; two hands, one foot bridges; side bridges with right hand and right foot. Boys go under each bridge as it is formed. Next, girls form partner bridges with hands and then with feet, and boys go under. Now it is the boys' turn to form all the bridges and girls go under each one as it is formed.

Student Bridges

WEEK 27

WARM-UP

Promotes: Abdominal strength, spatial awareness.

Activity:

(1) *Cross curl-ups:* Student lies on back, brings left knee to chest, then with right shoulder touches left knee. Alternate knees and shoulders. Many students will have a difficult time with this but encourage students to get shoulders as close to knees as possible without straining.

Cross Curl-Ups

155

(2) *Scissors in air:* Student lies on back, first crosses legs in air, then arms in air and then both together in air in front of body.

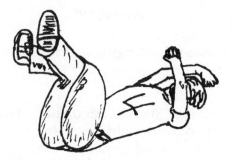

Scissors in Air

SCOOTER AND BALANCE BEAM

Promotes: Cooperation, dynamic balance, fun.

Need: Balance beam, two scooters, rope.

Activity:

(1) Student stands on balance beam and pulls rope. The end of the rope is held by a student on scooter. First student walks beam, pulling student on scooter. Student walks to end of beam, then changes places. Try pulling student using one hand (first right hand, then left).

(2) Student on beam walks beam pulling two students seated on scooters on each side of balance beam. (Students on scooters may need someone to help push.)

Activity #2

STEPPING STONES

Promotes: Gross motor coordination, motor planning.

Need: Stepping stones, beanbag.

Activity:

(1) Student tosses a beanbag on stones and hops to it in a hopscotch pattern of hop, jump, hop, jump, etc.

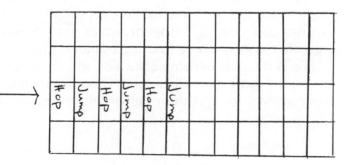

Activity #1

(2) *Skip:* Very slowly, a student hops and steps alternately through the stepping stones. Rhythm may be achieved by older students. Remember the rhythm: step left, hop on it, then step right, hop on it, etc.

JUMP BOX AND LADDER

Promotes: Fun, coordination, spatial awareness, self-confidence.

Need: Jump box, ladder leaning on box for incline position.

Activity:

(1) Student crawls up backward on rungs of ladder, sits on top of jump box facing ladder and slides backward down incline board to ground.

(2) Student walks up ladder with two feet and no hands, or with two hands and two feet (bear walk), and pulls body down incline board *on side.*

GAME

Activity:

Brownies and fairies: Students are divided into two groups at ends of room, one group of brownies and one of fairies. The brownies stand with backs turned to fairies and pretend to be asleep. The fairies, upon a quiet signal from teacher, try to sneak up on them. When the fairies get within a good distance for a chase, the teacher calls, "The fairies are coming." The brownies turn around and try gently to catch a fairy to bring home to brownie land. The captured fairies become brownies and the game continues until the fairies are all caught. Then the original brownies become fairies and the original fairies become brownies.

WEEK 28

Promotes: Creativity, cross-pattern awareness.

Activity:

(1) Students use whole body to create movement suggested by the following words: C—carry, crunch, crash, climb, collapse, circle, creep, cringe, crumble; D—dig, drop, disappear, dry, dog, dodge.

(2) With a partner, student makes his or her body into a "C" or "D." Try other letters of the alphabet; for example, the first letter in the student's name.

(3) *Partner claps:* Students sit facing partner, then clap right hand to right hand, left hand to left hand. Then, shake hands and rub hands together, always right to right, left to left.

Activity #2

STEPPING STONES

Promotes: Motor planning, cross-pattern awareness, gross motor coordination.

Need: Stepping stones.

Activity:

(1) *Indian dance:* Student hops four squares on right foot, left arm extended straight in front, then hops four squares on left foot, right arm extended straight in front of body. Student develops a rhythm and continues to end of stones.

(2) *Forward strides:* Student places hands on hips, stands with one foot forward and one foot back to stride position. Student jumps forward one square and alternates feet. Pattern continues to end of stones.

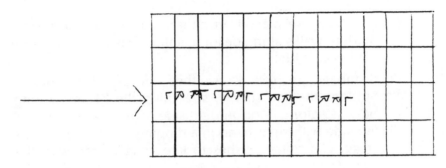

Forward Strides

LADDER

Promotes: Motor planning, gross motor coordination, spatial awareness.

Need: Ladder.

Activity:

(1) *Forward strides with clap:* Student jumps forward between rungs with first one foot forward and then the other foot forward, clapping with each jump.

(2) *Movement patterns:* Student moves along ladder in the following patterns: (a) jump, jump, hop; (b) jump, hop; (c) student creates own pattern and teaches the pattern to class. Remind students about movement patterns resembling sets, and challenge them to create an ABC pattern or an ABB pattern. For example, an ABC would be jump, hop, skip and an ABB would be step, jump, jump.

BALANCE BEAM

Promotes: Eye/hand coordination, directionality, dynamic balance.

Need: Balance beam, two beanbags, balloon, yardstick.

Activity:

(1) Beanbags are placed on either side of balance beam. Student walks along beam pushing beanbag along floor with a yardstick.

(2) Beanbags are placed on either side of balance beam. Student sits and scoots, straddling the beam pushing beanbag along floor on right side with left hand and on left side with right hand in a dipping movement. Stress small, controlled pushes to keep bag in line with the beam.

(3) Student walks along beam, pushing balloon along floor with yardstick.

COOPERATIVE GAME

Activity:

Relays: Students are divided evenly into two groups that stand in lines facing one another from opposite ends of the room. First student from each line slides to the center of the room, meets other student, joins hands and jumps two times. Then they part and run to the end of their lines. Second student from each line repeats action and game continues until all students have had a chance to slide and jump.

Variation: Students walk in giant steps or baby steps to center of room. They may skip to the center and clap hands two times or swing with elbows locked in a square-dance manner. (*Hint:* Students love relays! Relays are even more fun when the teacher stresses team effort and gives students the idea that everybody wins by getting good exercise.)

WEEK 29

Promotes: Form perception, concept of fixation.

Activity:

(1) Students use mouth, arms, legs, fingers, to form a variety of shapes. (Example: Make circles with arms, triangles with fingers, then arms.)

Activity #1

(2) Students draw large *overlapping* circles in front of body with arms. Right arm goes clockwise, left arm goes counterclockwise. *Focus eyes* in center where circles overlap. Then reverse directions.

(3) Students point to shapes in room: windows, ceiling, lights, pictures, floor tiles, door knobs, etc., and to shapes on clothes they are wearing.

LADDER

Promotes: Gross motor coordination, motor planning, spatial awareness.

Need: Ladder suspended on chairs approximately two feet off floor.

Activity:

(1) One student may sit on end of ladder on chair to steady it during this lesson. Second student climbs over and under rungs on ladder.

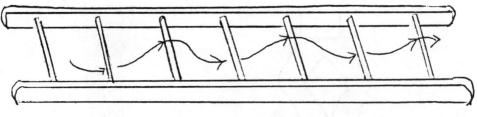

Activity #1

(2) Student crawls and then bear walks (with hands and feet on rungs) over rungs.

(3) Mature students may walk on ladder with two students on each side of ladder acting as safety patrol.

SCOOTER ON STEPPING STONES

Promotes: Form perception, gross motor coordination.

Need: Stepping stones, scooter.

Activity:

(1) Student walks in pattern forming shapes of a square, triangle, circle, and rectangle on stones.

(2) Student sits on scooter on stepping stones and moves in shapes of a circle, triangle, square and then around the outer edges of the stepping stones to form a rectangle.

NOTE: *Teacher can also use masking tape or rope to make shapes in stepping stones if students cannot perceive shapes.*

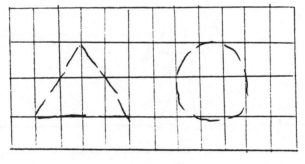

Activity #2

BALANCE BEAM

Promotes: Eye/hand coordination, dynamic balance, cooperation.

Need: Balance beam, balloon on string.

Activity:

(1) Student walks quickly on balance beam pulling balloon behind, over head, to his or her sides.

(2) Student plays catch with friend *on beam* while walking on beam.

(3) Student bats balloon in front of self while walking quickly on beam. The balloon is held in one hand while batting with other. (*Hint:* Balloon has a string tied to it so students will have success batting balloon instead of chasing it.)

Activity #3

GAME

Activity:

Go round the block: Students stand in one large circle. One student is chosen to be "It" and that student walks around the circle. "It" stops between two students and taps them on the shoulder. They run in opposite directions around the circle trying to be the first one back to their place. The first one back becomes "It" and the game continues. When "It" chooses two students, the rest of the class chants: "_____Nikki_____ (name of a student), run around the block, _____Lynette_____ (name of another student), try to beat the clock!"

WEEK 30

WARM-UP

Promotes: Happy faces, creativity.

Activity:

(1) Students make a smile (semicircle) with fingers, one arm, two arms, mouth, one leg, two legs, and finally with whole body.

(2) Two students stand face to face holding hands and swinging arms back and forth. Sing, "The more we swing together, together, together, the more we swing together, the happier we will be." Try to turn around without letting go of hands.

(3) Students, facing each other, hold right hands together and left hands together and try to turn outward without letting go of hands.

LADDER

Promotes: Cooperation, gross motor coordination, motor planning.

Need: Ladder, tiny bell.

Activity:

(1) Two students stand face to face, each in separate space between rungs of ladder holding hands. Both students jump between rungs. One student will be jumping forward and the other backward. Young students enjoy playing follow the leader down the ladder.

169

(2) Two students stand facing each other, one on each side of ladder rails, and jump inside ladder rails, then outside ladder rails. Repeat to end of ladder. Students will be jumping forward into ladder and backward out of ladder. First one student jumps and makes room for partner. Then partner jumps. Students could also stride rungs if desired.

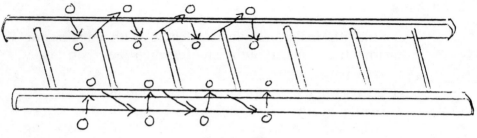

Activity #2

STEPPING STONES

Promotes: Cross-pattern awareness, gross motor coordination.

Need: Stepping stones.

Activity:

(1) *Cross over:* Student stands with one foot in each square. Student steps through stones and crosses left foot ahead to square in front of right; then right foot crosses ahead to square in front of left foot.

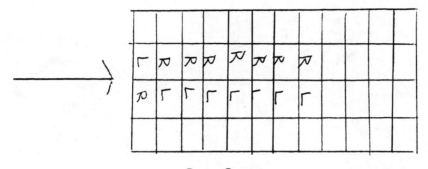

Cross Over

(2) *The scoot:* Student sits on square with knees to chest, arms holding knees. Student extends both legs and slides hips toward heels. Student continues scooting in this manner throughout stepping stones.

(3) *Hip walk:* Student sits on square with legs extended in front of body and hip-walks forward by shifting weight from one side of body to the other. Each leg scoots forward a little as weight is shifted.

BALANCE BEAM

Promotes: Cooperation, tactile awareness, gross motor coordination.

Need: Balance beam.

Activity:

(1) Three students stand sideways on beam holding hands while another student crawls between students' hands and under their legs.

(2) Four students lie on their backs, two on each side of balance beam. Students make bridges over the beam with toes touching each other. Hold while another student creeps under bridges with tummy on beam.

Activity #1

Activity #2

Challenge:

(1) Repeat Activities #1 and #2 with student moving backward between students on balance beam and along balance beam.

GAME

Activity:

Bubble gum, bubble gum, in a dish (sugarless, of course): Students stand in one large circle holding hands. One student is "It" standing in center. Students shake hands while chanting, "Bubble gum, bubble gum, in a dish. How many pieces do you wish?" "It" says a number, such as "4." Students stomp feet and count, "one, two, three, four, POP." On "POP," all students run until "It" tags someone. That person becomes the next "It" and the game begins again.

WEEK 31

WARM-UP

Promotes: Static balance, creativity.

Activity:

(1) Student kneels on both knees then lifts right knee off floor and holds ankle of elevated right knee. Puts opposite arm out for support.

(2) Students make the shape of the letter "E" with their bodies in as many ways as possible. Then students act out these "E" words: egg beater, egg, elephant, energy, and elevator.

LADDER

Promotes: Counting skills, gross motor coordination.

Need: Ladder, cards with numbers one through ten placed between rungs, beanbag.

Activity:

(1) *Number jumping:* Student jumps to space between rungs with one jump and jumps in place the correct number of jumps as indicated by the cards. Students may clap hands and count out loud as desired.

(2) Student puts beanbag between knees and jumps from space to space between rungs.

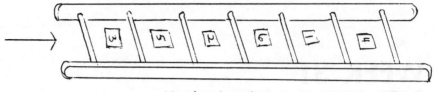

Number Jumping

BALANCE BEAM

Promotes: Dynamic balance, cross-pattern awareness, motor planning.

Need: Balance beam, beanbag.

Activity:

(1) *Bucking bronco:* Student crouches, puts hands and feet on beam and *one at a time* kicks feet up above back level and lands on beam. Then student moves hands several inches forward and walks feet forward and repeats kicks. Student should have at least three sets of kicks along beam.

(2) Student steps on right foot on left side of beam and pushes the beanbag (placed on the floor) along the floor with the left foot. The left foot steps on the right side of the beam and the right foot crosses over the beam to push the bag along the floor, placing the right foot on the left side. Continue to end of beam.

ROPE

Promotes: Cross-pattern awareness, gross motor coordination, cooperation.

Need: Rope.

Activity:

(1) Two students hold ends of rope about six to twelve inches off ground. Third student hurdles over rope. To accomplish the hurdle, student runs to rope, extends one arm in front of body and takes off and lands on the opposite foot. Each student should have several hurdles with the rope at a reasonable height.

(*Hint:* Jumping frightens some students so place rope low enough where it will be comfortable to them.)

COOPERATIVE GAME

Activity:

(1) *Flying angel:* Students choose a partner. First student sits on floor with legs up at a 45-degree angle. Second student places chest on feet of first student and leans slowly forward, keeping back straight, arms out, head up. Both hold the position for a count of five, and then change positions.

(2) *Triangle balance:* Two students lie on backs and raise feet to meet in air between bodies, with legs and knees straight. They hold for a count of five.

Triangle Balance

Low Bridge

(3) *Low bridge:* One student lies on stomach, then assumes a crawling position with weight on knees and hands. Second student lies on stomach at right angle and places legs on bottom of first student. Second student uses arms to support back while trying to attain a posture with a straight back. They hold for a count of five, then change positions.

WEEK 32

Promotes: Cross-lateral awareness, shoulder strength, concept of fixation.

Activity:

(1) *Wall press:* Students stand facing wall, arm's distance away. Student chooses spot (on wall) on which to fixate and places hands at shoulder level on wall. Student keeps eyes on spot and slowly leans in, legs and knees straight until nose touches spot and then stands straight. Repeat ten times.

(2) Students stand facing wall, arm's distance away and lean straight arms on wall. Students raise right arm and left leg, then return to standing position. Then they raise left arm and right leg, and return to original position. Students raise each set of arms and legs five times.

(3) *Kicks:* Students stand facing wall, arm's distance away and lean in to put nose on spot. Students hold this position and alternately kick legs backward. Have them try sets of five for each leg.

SCOOTERS

Promotes: Coordination, cooperation, arm strength.

Need: Two scooters and three cones.

Activity:

(1) Teacher places two scooters side by side. Two students sit on scooters and hold inside hands. They use free hand to push the scooters around the cones. Students hold hands until they have gone around cones, then change hands for the trip back to the beginning. (If student pushed with the left hand, change to the right while holding hands with the left.) Some students may prefer a rope or scarf to keep them in touch with their partners.

Scoot with a Friend

STEPPING STONES

Promotes: Cross-lateral awareness, eye/hand coordination.

Need: Stepping stones.

Activity:

(1) *Grapevine with hands:* Student stands at left end facing side of stepping stones and places both hands in one square. Student moves right hand to the right side one square and crosses left hand over right hand to land in same square (to right of right hand). Now right hand moves to the right side one square and left hand crosses under right hand to land in same square (to right of right hand). Student continues pattern of "side-over-side-back" to end of stepping stones.

(2) Repeat above activity facing side of stepping stones and using hands and feet to perform grapevine. Remember: "Side-over-side-back!"

BALANCE BEAM

Promotes: Directionality, balance, spatial awareness.

Need: Balance beam, ball.

Activity:

(1) Student holds ball high above head using both hands and makes full turns while walking across the beam. Student's center of gravity is raised in this activity because the arms are extended. Balance is challenged, so remind students to turn slowly.

(2) London Bridge: Two students make bridge with hands or a hoop over the balance beam while remainder of group moves across the beam in any fashion they choose. When bridge falls, student on beam takes a turn being the bridge. Keep rotating until all get a chance to walk and be a part of the bridge.

London Bridge

GAME

Need: Scarfs or handkerchiefs.

Activity:

Raise the Flag: Students stand in two lines facing each other. One student stands in the middle between both lines with shoulders pointing at each group. This student is the flag pole which has two flags, the scarfs. When the flags are down, the flag pole's arms are at sides and students in lines are crouched down. As flags are raised, class slowly stands until flags are at top and lines are standing tall. Next flag pole lowers flags and then raises them alternately, stopping at each position: part way up, half way up, etc. Students in lines must watch the flag on their side in order to move to the proper position! Change turns so as many students as possible may be the flags.

Raise the Flag

APPENDIX
OF GAMES AND
OTHER ACTIVITIES

GAMES

WARM-UPS

STEPPING-STONES ACTIVITIES

LADDER ACTIVITIES

BALANCE-BEAM ACTIVITIES

STUNTS

BIBLIOGRAPHY

Arnold, Arnold. *The World Book of Children's Games*. New York: World Publishings, 1972.

Capon, Jack. *Perceptual Motor Lesson Plans*. Alameda, California: Front Row Publishers, 1971.

Cratty, Bryant J. *Movement Behavior and Motor Learning, 2nd ed*. Philadelphia: Lea and Febiger, 1967.

Gilliom, Bonnie Cherp. *Basic Movement Education for Children: Rationale and Teaching Units*. Reading, Massachusetts: Addison-Wesley Publishing Company, 1970.

Langhorts, Emma and McPherson, Marie. *Action in Learning*. Oaklawn, Illinois: Ideal School Supply Company, 1974.

Orlick, Terry. *The Cooperative Sports and Games Book*. New York: Pantheon Books, 1978.

Pulaski, Mary Ann Spencer. *Understanding Piaget*. New York: Harper and Row, 1971.

Werner, Peter and Rini, Lisa. *Perceptual Motor Development Equipment*. West Nyack, New York: Parker Publishing Company, Inc., 1974.

———. Foundations and Practices in Perceptual Motor Learning. Washington, D.C.: AAHPER Publications, 1971.

———. Perceptual Motor Program. Boise, Idaho: Boise Public Schools, 1974.

INDEX

A

Agility, 16, 52, 57
Airplane, 43, 47
Angels in the snow, 47
Arm circles, 31
Arm strength, 81
Auditory acuity, 16, 43, 44
Awareness of side:
    left, 99, 113
    right, 86, 97, 98, 113

B

Balance, 31, 33, 36, 47, 85
    dynamic, 40, 44, 48, 58, 89
    static, 65
Balance beam activities (table),
    194
Balance beam circles, 112
Balance beam fire drill, 59
Ball, 44, 46, 54, 56, 57, 90, 91,
    98, 109, 110
Ball drop, 95
Balloon, 90, 99, 166
Beads, 94
Beanbag, 49–51, 62, 63, 82,

Beanbag (*cont.*)
    108, 112, 136, 137, 151, 157,
    162, 175, 176
Beanbag headache, 82
Beanbag twist, 50
Bear on the move, 105
Bear walk, 71
Bell, 93
Bibliography, 197
Bicycle, 143
Bicycle tires (see hoops)
Balloon, blowing up pretend, 34
Big jump, little jump, 36
Bilateral, 12, 16, 23, 29
Body control, 33
Body division, 129
Body image, 31, 35, 48, 51, 65
Body shapes, 163
Bronco, 41, 42
Brownies and fairies, 158
Bubble gum, bubble gum in a
    dish, 173
Bucking bronco, 176
Bunny hop, 37, 56, 64, 79
    song, 38
Burpee, 32